The Partnered Po[r]

What is Possible, Practical and Powerful with Small Equ[ines]

Jenifer Morrissey
Willowtrail Farm
Gould, Colorado
2015

ISBN-13: 978-0692580240
ISBN-10: 0692580247

Published by
Willowtrail Farm
P.O. Box 1034
Walden, CO 80480
www.willowtrailfarm.com
in conjunction with createspace.com
and available at
www.amazon.com

DEDICATION

This book is dedicated to my ponies,
especially
Mya the Wonder Pony and
Norwegian Fjord gelding OH Torrin,
who've shown just how much is possible with ponies.

With sincere thanks to Patricia Burge of Lost Creek Ranch who mentored me as I was beginning my pony journey, found Mya the Wonder Pony for me, and introduced me to my first Fell Ponies.

ACKNOWLEDGEMENTS

My life with ponies would not be possible without the support of my husband Don Ewy who helps with chores and more importantly finds places the ponies can contribute in our business. I am grateful to my former husband Tom Morrissey who supported my initial foray into equine pursuits. I also appreciate the support of my friends Dina Bennett and Bernard Gateau and my neighbors Kirk Peck and the late Melissa Malcolm-Peck.

In addition to Pat Burge, I am grateful to many pony friends who understand about the working heritage of ponies. My Fell Pony mentor Joe Langcake has generously shared from his many decades of knowledge that began with training pit ponies. My Lancashire friend Eddie McDonough has a keen nose for working pony lore and generously shares it with me, patiently waiting for his finds to appear somewhere in my writings. I am grateful to Judith Bean whose lifelong love of the Fell Pony gives her great perspective. In Germany I am grateful to Antje Assheuer for her friendship and interest in partnering with ponies.

ANTJE'S PONY HELENA HELPING

iv

CREDITS

The stories "Irony of Skidding in Teller City" and "Stewarding the Hooves of Horses" were first published in different form in *Rural Heritage* magazine.

The story "Right Mind, Right Body" was previously published in different form in *Fell Ponies: Observations on the Breed, the Breed Standard, and Breeding* by the author.

Portions of the story "On the Job Versatility Testing" were previously published in *Savvy Times, Fjord Herald,* and *Rural Heritage.*

The story "Wildfire Mitigation" was first published in different form in *Fjord Herald.*

The garden cart portion of "Pony-Powered Garden and ATV Carts" was co-authored with Tom Morrissey.

Before I purchased a camera with a self-timer, I was indebted to my husband Don Ewy and former husband Tom Morrissey for taking pictures of me with my ponies.

I am grateful to Jim Buzzard, Katie Currier, Wendy Francisco, Margi Greene, Paula Guenther, Jill Page, and April Whicker for contributing photographs to this work.

A FEW WORDS ABOUT SAFETY

Working with equines - ponies and otherwise - can be dangerous. In the end, no one can keep you safe but you and your own good judgment. There may be photographs in this book that show the author riding without a helmet or not holding the lines when working in harness. This book does not advocate these practices. You should own the responsibility for your own safety and that of your pony.

THANKFUL FOR MY PONIES 2011

I'm thankful for my ponies
Who've been so patient with me
While I have been away from them
More than I wanted to be.

They're wanting time and stimulation,
And they're offering ideas of their own.
They want opportunities to be with me
As they've repeatedly shown.

There's the one I've taught to shake her hoof;
She offers when I come to her gate.
There's the one that always asks questions.
Any answer from me is great!

There's the one who follows me about
To see if I'll give her a scratch.
There's one when I have a halter
Makes himself very easy to catch.

There's the one that gently nickers
Whenever I appear.
That sound is definitely something
That leaves me in good cheer.

There's one that wants acknowledgement.
A treat will do just fine.
A handful of hay is what another wants.
I'm mostly an excuse to dine.

These ponies that I love
Have definitely missed my attention.
I love them more for these games they play
And others I've forgotten to mention.

I'm thankful for my ponies
And the creativity that they show
In finding ways to engage me.
From here it's exciting to think where we'll go.

CONTENTS

FORWARD: WHAT IS A PARTNERED PONY?

Different people think of the word 'partner' in different ways with respect to equines. For some it is the beginning step in a path of horsemanship. For me, it is not a step. Rather it is a way of being with equines that anyone can adopt at any level of training. And while benefits accrue to a pony who is partnered, there are at least as many if not more benefits that accrue to the human side of the equation. My experience has been exclusively with equines shorter than fourteen hands high. I'm sure, though, that it's possible to partner fully with a large 'pony' as well. From my study, the same principles apply.

So what is a partnered pony? It's a pony whose human wants a shared life with their equine. It's a pony whose human makes choices so that the pony wants that shared life, too. It's a pony whose human makes choices that maximize the pony's <u>desire</u> to participate in that shared life. It's a pony whose human makes choices that maximize the pony's <u>ability</u> to participate in that shared life. A partnered pony is fortunate, but its human partner is even more so.

It's endless what partnering with a pony can look like: work, play, shows, chores, training, feeding, tack/harness, commuting, celebration, recreation, competition, riding, driving, packing, draft work. Every pony-person-partnership will have their own list unique to them.

Ponies have an undeserved bad reputation. People fail to understand a pony's desire to be more than a pet or a lawn ornament or a companion for a larger equine. Most ponies want to live life to its fullest. There are at least seven common misunderstandings about ponies. You'll read about them later. Maybe you'll come up with some pony myths of your own.

My first exposure to the idea of a partnered pony was reading works of fiction, but then I was introduced to Patricia Burge. With Pat, partnered ponies were a reality, not fiction. When I met her, Pat was immediately generous with her time and knowledge. I don't know how many trips I made to Lost Creek Ranch where Pat and her husband Dick welcomed me to learn by watching and helping where I could. While there were horses there, it was the ponies that I found most interesting.

My life with ponies would not be what it is were it not for what Pat showed me at my beginning. Since then I've met others, especially in the Fell Pony community, who have partnered ponies. I've included short stories about them, too, as examples of what other pony-person-partnerships look like.

Every pony is unique, and every person is unique. And exactly how a particular pony and a particular person partner will be unique, too. How I partner with Mya the Wonder Pony or my Fjord Horse Torrin is different from how Pat has partnered with

her ponies Tugboat and Moonshine and Danny, as you'll read. My hope is that by sharing from my experience, as Pat did with me, you'll want to partner with a pony or expand your current partnership.

My life has been with ponies and horses of all kinds since I left Alaska at age 11. My childhood there was filled with rehabilitating wildlife and dreaming of a future doing the same for horses.

Ponies can indeed be partners as Jenifer describes. Years ago, I bought many simple ponies from the kill buyer. They all developed in positive ways and were sold with a guarantee I would take them back if they did not suit the buyer. No pony came back! But I did receive photos and happy comments.

The three ponies whose stories I will share were special partners for a number of years and changed my life forever. Each of those ponies partnered with me in the disciplines of riding, driving, chore helping, and developing truly delightful personalities; they were there to be partnered with! There is such a striking difference between MoonShine as my mountain and valley steed of keen judgment and courage, Tugboat as my around-the-ranch transport, and Danequiel as my magical steed that made people dream and feel joy.

I've always been drawn to equines on the edge. Although I have raised and trained some rare breeds, I've always had a special place in my heart for rejected equines, no matter their breeding status. Today it is the plight of mustangs on our public lands that concerns me. We need desperately to help bring about a humane solution.

In my experience working with mustangs, they have that strong pony personality. When they can trust you, they bond strongly, and for me, they have done everything I have ever asked them to do.

My first mustang was wild and would never step on or over anything, let alone consider a rider. In the wild he was a vigilant survivor. He learned to trust me, and I him. He would jump anything I asked. He was a small horse, and still jumped big. We both had youth and spunk, and I let him decide how to jump the jumps! We were Reserve Champion Jumper of the year at National Western Stock Show.

The best way for people to experience the qualities that ponies have, if they can't be with them in person, is to hear their stories. You will find here many stories that may help you know ponies better.

Preparing my stories for this book has given me precious time to rejoice over the memories of the ponies I've loved, and to grieve over MoonShine's loss of sight and Tugboat's and Danequiel's loss of presence. They are there as stars in the sky.

Patricia Burge
Lost Creek Ranch, 2015

INTRODUCTION

My father Bob Simpson sometimes referred to himself as Scotty McSimpson. He did this because he felt the Scottish part of his ancestry made him forever look for ways to avoid spending money. My version of that inheritance seems to be forever looking for ways to accomplish multiple goals while using the fewest resources. That is how I came to love ponies. They are able to do so many different things, and they are relatively easy to keep. Perfect!

I first learned about the versatility of ponies by reading works of fiction. Some equestrians think of versatility as multiple different riding disciplines or perhaps multiple different types of driving. For me, though, the novels of Jean Auel aptly illustrated that versatility goes way beyond riding and driving. Her books included a small equine who was used for riding, packing, and draft work (pulling a travois.) The pony was gentled from a wild state, and in addition to practical uses, the pony provided companionship to the heroine. Training was accomplished in a spirit of partnership.

When I got to a point in my life when I could have an equine of my own, I was fortunate to meet Pat Burge. Pat and her husband Dick demonstrated the sort of partnership that I had read about in Auel's novels. When Pat found my first pony for me, it never occurred to me to approach being with Mya any differently.

In hindsight it is perhaps remarkable that I've been able to involve my ponies in so much of what I do. Yet what I have done has been a natural extension of what I read about, what I saw Pat and Dick do, and in the end, what my ponies agreed to.

Along the way I found that they seem to enjoy and even crave being involved. In turn I enjoy what we do more, too. Our work together has taught me what is possible and what is practical. I've also been humbled by what my ponies have offered. Sometimes, it's pretty powerful.

Of course, partnering with ponies isn't new or modern. Most pony breeds were created or evolved specifically to provide all-around assistance to their human keepers. One equine that could be gainfully employed all week for work then taken to town on market day or to church on worship day was just practical, as was its ability to breed its own replacement.

I have found, as have many others over the ages, that it is indeed possible to use a single pony for riding, driving, draft work, and packing, as well as variations on all these themes. For me, riding has meant herding cows, checking fence, and ponying a new gelding to keep his incision open and draining, among other things. Driving has included runs to the mailbox, giving someone a pony cart ride, and accustoming a pony in training to the sight and sound of a wheeled vehicle. Draft work has included skidding logs, hauling manure, and bringing in firewood. Packing has looked like bringing in boughs for a holiday greens business, transporting tools to an off-road job site, and hauling materials to a back country location. I know much more is possible.

Of course ponies are smaller than today's typical working equines, so there are practical considerations, not the least of which is giving a pony every opportunity to maximize conversion of their motion to moving a load. Finding or making appropriately sized equipment is often required, for example. In addition, many pony breeds have good feet and are able to work barefoot, so learning to trim hooves properly (or at least learning what proper trimming looks like) helps keep expenses down as well as efficiency up. And speaking of hooves, pony owners are always aware of their partners' weight, since these smaller equines can have a propensity for founder. Involving them in our lives as much as possible keeps them active and engaged and less likely to become overweight and develop health issues.

I've heard, and I believe it to be true, that ponies, pound for pound, can outpull larger equines. To make this come true, then, as their partners, we humans have to give them every practical advantage possible. We must make sure the tack we use is safe and comfortable and adjusted for maximum efficiency, whether pack or riding saddles or draft or driving harness. We must make sure hooves are trimmed so movement is again safe and comfortable. Even when breeding replacements we must take care to choose proper conformation for the work at hand.

And then there is what is powerful, and I'm not talking about physical strength. There are times with ponies that are, for lack of a better word, profound. They will communicate, in some way, encouragement or appreciation or willingness or advice that we might not expect from a being that cannot speak in words like we do. Usually the communication is so well timed as to clearly not be a coincidence.

My involvement with ponies followed my interest in managing landscapes. If we are lucky enough to have stewardship responsibility for a small place, ponies can be very appropriate partners. It may take some willingness and imagination to figure out how to involve them. We may feel alone sometimes and feel like we have to invent solutions constantly. Because every pony, every person, and every place is different, it's likely that indeed our situation is unique. However, it's also likely that someone has done something similar with a pony at some time somewhere, and by telling stories here, perhaps I can alleviate loneliness, offer possible solutions, and maybe even spark creativity.

In the next few pages, you'll read some examples of pony-person-partnerships. Each partnership looks different because the pony-person pair is unique.. Christine Robinson, for instance, set out to prove, successfully, that ponies can do what horses can in many of the human-created equestrian endeavors. Along the way she also did a great variety of things with her pony Duke. Judith Bean and her pony are not only life partners but business partners, helping young and older do everything from take their first ride to compete in dressage. Eddie McDonough has found a wide variety of jobs for his pony Bess over the years, forging a partnership based on profound mutual respect.

Ultimately, my aim in sharing all of these stories is to encourage partnering with ponies because there is so much that is possible, because they are practical, and it can be profound. It's my hope that others will discover what I have: that one lifetime isn't enough.

CHRISTINE ROBINSON ON PONIES AS THE ORIGINAL ATVS

I was lucky enough to grow up with people who worked their horses. I got to do everything – fencing, hauling, herding sheep and cattle, and helping break ponies to ride and drive. My grandfather bought me my first pony when I was eight. Silver was a grey Welsh pony. He was kept at a stable. My parents weren't too happy because they thought I was too young. But I never looked back. I wanted a Fell Pony from the time I was eleven or twelve, but I was constantly told you couldn't do anything with them, meaning dressage or hunting or pony club. I just set off to show them wrong.

My first Fell Pony stallion was named Frizington Duke. I test-rode Duke in the middle of a housing estate, and he wasn't bothered, so I bought him. He was four years old. He became my favorite pony of all time. We did so much together. We literally did everything. Once I drove him to a show then we competed that day under saddle, working hunter and driven. I rode and drove him at home for pleasure, took hay to the mares on him, took him hunting once or twice a week in season, and did pony club games. It was easy to compete him driving because he didn't need a groom; he was that well behaved. I qualified him for National Pony Society (Britain) national driving champion one year. There wasn't anything he couldn't do.

In April 2010 five of my ponies and I helped the National Trust with path repair work. We carried 150 bags 3 ½ miles up 1411 vertical feet. The path repair team subsequently filled the bags and airlifted them into place. Working like this is what these ponies are bred for. They are the original ATV and you can see the pleasure they get from working.

Beginning in 2010, my ponies have done a very different kind of work. As conservation grazers, their job is to keep down the shrubs and coarse grass to keep the habitat suitable for rare butterflies to breed. I have no idea what my ponies and I might do next, but I'm sure they'll do well. They're all-rounders!

Christine Robinson is the breeder of the Kerbeck Fell Ponies and has served for more than twenty years on the Council of the Fell Pony Society in England.

EDDIE AND BESS

Bess is Eddie McDonough's twenty-two year old Fell Pony mare. She is stabled a few miles away from where Eddie lives. Eddie checks on Bess twice a day and sees her more often if they're working. Over the years, the work has always varied. She helps with herding sheep, she harrows pastures and paddocks, she snigs Christmas trees, and packs hay to sheep. She has also been known to protect Eddie from attacking dogs and aggressive equines.

When Eddie was considering purchasing a pony, he visited Bess at her previous owner's. "We've been waiting for you to show up," they said. Bess isn't your average easy-going pony, and they knew Eddie's background in working animals and his ability to turn around challenging cases would suit Bess well.

Bess has never been one to court affection; she's not interested in petting, for instance, and she's been known to kick a feed bucket up onto the roof of the stable. Eddie

calls her a hard-nosed work animal. Where she is housed, there are 60 equines and lots of traffic to go with them. Yet somehow Bess knows when Eddie is coming and she sheds her aloofness, whinnying a greeting before Eddie even comes in view.

Once they were many miles out on a drive over rough country, and they smashed the wheel of the trap. Bess never panicked; she just stood waiting for Eddie to figure out how to get them rolling again. Another time Eddie really tested their partnership. They had lost a sheep, and the pasture was too water-logged for a quad bike, so Eddie took Bess out in her harness to drag the carcass in. "I could tell she didn't like the assignment. Her ears were twitching constantly. The smell was enough to let her know it wasn't a job she wanted. I talked her through it. I wouldn't have even attempted it without a blinkered bridle. She would never have done it in an open bridle."

Eddie says Bess thrives on mutual understanding. "When you have a true partnership, when things get challenging, the pony knows you'll get things sorted out; ponies more so than horses," says Eddie. "There's something there; they're not a machine. And with Bess, I know she'll sort things too if necessary. She hasn't courted affection, but she's given me everything I've wanted in a working partner."

Eddie McDonough lives in Lancashire in England where he and his genuine working bearded collies help friends tend flocks of sheep and herds of cattle.

JUDITH'S STORY ABOUT LETTY

My twenty-two-year-old pony, a black 13.2hh Fell mare, and I are partners. Business partners, pleasure and managerial partners. Whatever work I require of her, she does with eagerness, quiet, and joy. We trust one another, enjoying each other's company.

Raisburn Letty II is my second Fell. In my childhood in Cumbria, homeland for centuries of Fell Ponies, I rode Linnel Buzzard in Pony Club, agricultural shows, up and down rocky mountains. I learnt much, too, from a local shepherd who drove and packed his ponies – all Fells.

After flying from England to Canada then coming to Maine, my Letty now enjoys teaching little girls to ride, jump, and show. A day without work is okay, but this pony comes to my call, asking "what are we doing today?"

I've done all her training myself. I can enjoy her personality, her tantrums in the pasture when snow falls off the barn roof, while trusting her to behave politely while working. I trust her work ethic, her ground manners, and her humor. Letty is a gem.

FIRST, LET'S STEP BACK

Before we dive into more stories about ponies and what is possible, practical, and powerful, let's first step back and look at some topics in the bigger picture.

There are lots of reasons why you might be hesitant to partner with a pony or might think you're not able to do so. To help, I'll address some common misconceptions about ponies and share what the famous clinician Monty Roberts has said about ponies. I'll even let the incomparable sleuth Sherlock Holmes weigh in on how ponies are different.

Next I'll talk about the very human problem of having time and resources for an expensive hobby like a pony, including a story letting you know that you're not alone. You'll also read that one of the keys to making it both work and be worthwhile is recognizing that every minute you're with your pony should be considered a positive investment.

From there I'll help you understand that it's the breadth of what ponies can do that makes them special. Finally I'll talk more seriously about a versatile piece of machinery than can put a partnered pony at risk.

21

SEVEN THINGS YOU'VE HEARD ABOUT PONIES
THAT AREN'T (NECESSARILY) TRUE

I don't know about you, but when I look at equine magazines, equine training videos, and equine books, more often than not I see horses … I don't see ponies. It seems to me that ponies have an undeserved bad reputation. Sometimes when I look at magazines, videos, and books, I might even see minis in addition to horses, but I don't see ponies. Minis, of course, are miniature horses, not miniature ponies, a distinction that anyone involved with minis will certainly tell you to make sure the bad rep of ponies doesn't fall on minis.

As someone who's partnered with ponies for nearly two decades, there's a lot I hear about ponies that just doesn't match my experience. For instance, I've heard that ponies are:

1. Small
2. Lazy and/or stubborn
3. Mean
4. Just for kids
5. Not for serious undertakings
6. (Just) A little horse
7. All the same (if you've seen one pony you've seen them all)

Because I breed ponies, I occasionally get people asking if the ponies I breed have the bad characteristics so often attributed to ponies. My very first exposure to a pony helps me understand where these sorts of questions are coming from. As a child I was enamored with all things equine, and when I was about ten years old, a neighbor friend had permission to visit and ride a pony belonging to another neighbor. On a few occasions, my friend would take me along. The pony was kept by itself, and it definitely fit the

22

first five descriptors in the list (small, lazy, mean, just for kids, and not for serious undertakings). I suspect it was a Shetland, and I don't remember being bitten, but I remember being warned to be careful. I was never allowed to ride the pony; my friend had much more equestrian experience than I did and even she had trouble getting the pony to do what she wanted it to do (jumping a rail, for instance).

My childhood equine experiences after that short-lived exposure to a pony were entirely with horses. I then took a twenty-five year break from equestrian pursuits, ending when I got my first pony. My early childhood experience gives me a little insight into the questions I get from people about the ponies that I breed. As I've pondered how to respond, I've come to some conclusions about why people believe things about ponies that aren't necessarily true.

1. PONIES ARE SMALL

When it comes to size, the general definition of a pony of course is anything 14.2hh or smaller. When compared to a 17hh warmblood or draft horse, yes it's true that 14hh is small. However, I often ask people why they think they need something that big. I will then help them understand, if applicable, that a 13hh pony may well be enough 'horse' for them to accomplish their goals. I have two examples of large pony breeds in my herd, and while visitors don't call them tall, they definitely do not call them small either because these ponies have bone and substance that many larger horses do not.

People often, of course, equate height with carrying capacity. However, hoof diameter and bone are probably better indicators of carrying capacity than height. And many of the large pony breeds have both bone and hoof sizes comparable to larger equines. A study I did on carrying capacity and a historical reflection about common gear hauled on large ponies suggests that many large ponies are up to carrying similar weight to Quarter Horses (in part because people are

23

breeding Quarter Horses with smaller feet than they really should). (1)

The smallest pony in my herd is 11.2hh. Mya definitely fits people's pre-conceived notions of a pony when it comes to size. There's something Mya has, though, that is bigger than many of the larger ponies: her work ethic. She'll outwork any of the rest of my herd. She's the pony we go to when we need something unusual done (like relocating rattlesnakes out of the barnyard). I can't think of a time when she's refused to work. So while people shake their heads in wonder when they see her in her work harness, they never question her willingness to get things done once they see her in action.

2. PONIES ARE LAZY AND/OR STUBBORN

I once watched a video that stated that a lot of horse training relies on shaping the flight instinct. When a smart, confident horse comes along that isn't as inclined to move its feet after being given the usual cues, these trainers often label the horse as lazy, stubborn or, worse, untrainable. This was a revelation to me; my introduction to horse training was based first on establishing a relationship of trust, then progressing to what looks more conventional in terms of riding and harness work.

This revelation about horse training via reliance on the flight instinct helps me understand a little better why many people don't like ponies since many ponies are quite smart and less inclined to move their feet. Getting their respect first is often necessary before they will cooperate with a human training agenda. Then a pony that at first appears lazy or stubborn can suddenly become one that will move its feet willingly. Perhaps instead of labeling ponies lazy or stubborn, it's the trainers who should be labeled that way because they aren't willing to change their training techniques to ones that work with a different sort of equine!

3. PONIES ARE MEAN

Have I been bit by one of my ponies? Yes. Did I deserve it? Yes, at least in their eyes, and with 20/20 hindsight I have to agree with them. Were they being mean? No. In the first instance that comes to mind, I was giving a pony a hug that doesn't like that sort of affection. In the second case, a stallion was being playful, and I wasn't paying enough attention to redirect his play drive.

I think ponies get a reputation for being mean for two reasons. First, if the pony is small, we may treat it like we would a pet - a dog or a cat for instance - like I did giving my pony a hug. Ponies are very different from dogs or cats, and in more ways than we might initially think. One of the big differences is often emphasized in natural horsemanship circles: ponies are prey animals and dogs and cats are predators. The way they interact with other species therefore differs. Do I have ponies whom I can give hugs to without being bitten? Yes, of course, and I can even give the pony that bit me a hug, too, now, though she still doesn't like it. But I've learned that the relationship I have with the object of my hug must be such that they can receive the hug not as a sign of domination or aggression but as 'a human thing.' Not all ponies or all relationships allow for that.

The second reason that I think ponies get a reputation for being mean is that we feed them in ways that create 'mean' behavior. I remember being on a picnic many years ago with friends. There were two kids under the age of ten, and midway through our meal, a thunderstorm arrived, and it began to rain suddenly and ferociously. We madly gathered our meal and headed for the minivan our friends had driven to the picnic area. Dessert that night was chocolate brownies with raspberry sauce. Within just five minutes of consuming dessert, the minivan became too small as the kids suddenly had more energy and play drive than was appropriate in that confined space. It was a stark illustration of the effect of sugar on behavior. While we may not feed chocolate brownies to ponies, in many cases people do feed sugar or close approximations thereof. Whether the sugar is in the form of a treat (peppermints anyone?) or in a molasses binder in a feed or in the form of grains of any kind (which can break down into simple sugars easily), I believe these foods can create behavior that could be considered mean (biting, kicking, etc.) Most ponies don't work hard enough to need concentrated feeds like this. In cases where extra calories are needed, low NSC feeds are more appropriate since they provide the energy without the problems inherent with grains and sweeteners.

Vitamins and minerals, or lack thereof, can also play a role in creating unwanted behavior. I've chosen to use one vitamin supplement over another made by the same company because of slight differences in behavior that I've detected. I also remember once when one of my stallions suddenly developed an edge to his temperament. After a few days of being puzzled, I realized I had let his minerals run out; unfortunately it had been more than a week since I had thought to check them. After a few days back on his minerals, his temperament was back to the calm and pleasant one I was used to. More often than not, then, I think we humans create mean ponies, either through how we treat them or how we feed them.

4. PONIES ARE JUST FOR KIDS

Unlike other countries, in the United States we do not have a native pony breed with a long history. In many other countries, ponies established themselves during the heyday of equine horsepower as willing partners used by adults to accomplish necessary work. It's therefore my belief that in America because of our lack of direct experience, we've assumed that ponies are just for kids because they're smaller than the horses that do have a working history here.

There are of course lots of adults in America who take an interest in ponies, though rarely in the mainstream equine pursuits. For instance, *Driving Digest* magazine reported in 2013 the following about the Kentucky Classic: "Fourteen classes spanning Preliminary through Advanced were filled with 56 entries. Almost two-thirds were pony entries. With nine Preliminary Pony entries and nine Preliminary Single Pony entries, pony power was exploding." (2) Ponies are prominent in advertisements in the magazine as well as in other articles

One of the other reasons I think we assume ponies are just for kids is that we have a fixed image of a pony, and it's a lot like a Shetland, relatively small. The larger and more substantial breeds of ponies just haven't been well known. As these breeds become better known and as the equestrian population ages, ponies are getting a second look by adults looking for mounts that are sensible of mind, sure-footed, and closer to the ground.

5. PONIES ARE NOT FOR SERIOUS UNDERTAKINGS

One of the most famous ponies that rose to the top of an equine sport was Seldom Seen, a Thoroughbred-Connemara cross. Standing at 14.2hh, this pony was the partner of Lendon Gray, and together they competed at the highest levels of dressage. "He won USDF Horse of the Year awards from Third Level through Grand Prix, as well as an individual gold medal at the U.S. Olympic Festival in Syracuse, NY…. The impressive pony was retired in 1987, after winning the Grand Prix, Grand Prix Special, and Grand Prix Freestyle at Dressage at Devon…. Although very small for a Grand Prix dressage horse, and described as an average mover, Seldom Seen was very successful, and was particularly loved by the public because he was an 'average' horse that performed spectacularly. The pony was inducted into the USDF Hall of Fame in 2005." (3)

COURTESY JIM BUZZARD

From the serious sport of dressage, now I'll give examples of serious work with ponies in the draft world. Haflingers and Fjords especially are often used for farm and forest work. (I consider these pony breeds; some people may classify them differently. I wish to be inclusive.) My friend Jim Buzzard has worked six Haflingers on a plow during spring, summer, and fall at various venues in the Midwest. And of course I have used my Fjord and my Shetland-Welsh cross for forest work in our logging business. Earning money professionally seems to me an indication that serious work is being done!

6. PONIES ARE A LITTLE HORSE

A phenotype is a set of outwardly observable physical characteristics. There is no question that some ponies have a horse phenotype, being a horse in a smaller package (Seldom Seen, described above, fits this category given that he's called both a horse and a pony in the discussion quoted from Wikipedia.) However there are a number of ponies that are quite distinct from the horse phenotype.

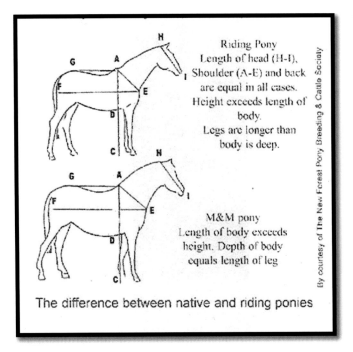

Riding Pony
Length of head (H-I),
Shoulder (A-E) and back
are equal in all cases.
Height exceeds length of
body.
Legs are longer than
body is deep.

M&M pony
Length of body exceeds
height. Depth of body
equals length of leg

By courtesy of The New Forest Pony Breeding & Cattle Society

The difference between native and riding ponies

The best illustration I have ever seen of this distinction comes from the New Forest Pony Breeding & Cattle Society. Their illustration contrasts 'riding ponies' from British Native or Mountain & Moorland Ponies. To my eye, 'riding ponies' have a horse phenotype, but native ponies are quite distinct from the larger equines. Wikipedia describes the pony phenotype this way: "Compared to other horses, ponies often exhibit thicker manes, tails and overall coat, as well as proportionally shorter legs, wider barrels, heavier bone, thicker necks, and shorter heads with broader foreheads." (4) Many pony breed societies become livid when their ponies are called 'mini' this-or-that-horse because such a description obscures the many traits that make their pony unique and distinguish it from other breeds.

7. PONES ARE ALL THE SAME

Jill Page breeds and trains Pony of the Americas (POA) ponies in Texas. She says people tell her all the time that they have a POA because their pony was born in America. Jill then must patiently explain that POAs are actually a distinct breed with a strict standard for admission for registration. Just because a pony is born in America doesn't make it a POA.

Wikipedia lists 109 breeds of ponies worldwide. (5) Until I got involved with British Native Ponies, I had no idea there were so many different kinds of ponies. When I was growing up, I only knew four: Shetland, Welsh, Connemara, and Chincoteague. Perhaps one of the reasons that the different breeds of ponies are not well known is that many of them are at risk of extinction. According to a genetic study done on several pony breeds, "...approximately 700 horse and pony populations are found worldwide. Of these populations, approximately 181 are listed to be at some risk of extinction, and another 272 are of unknown status. Many of the at-risk populations are pony breeds." (6)

While the word 'pony' has a distinct definition for many people, for others it is as general a term as 'horse' is. 'Pony' can be an affectionate term for any equine, or it can refer to a particular type of equine, such as a polo pony. From my perspective, the broadest possible definition of the term is the best one since I believe you have to treat a pony the way you should treat a horse. All members of the equine world would benefit if ponies were the norm rather than the exception!

COURTESY JILL PAGE

1) Morrissey, Jenifer. "Carrying Capacity," *Fell Ponies: Observations on the Breed, the Breed Standard, and Breeding.* Gould, Colorado: Willowtrail Farm, 2013, p. 90.
2) Pringle, Ann L. "Pony Power Explodes in Kentucky," *Driving Digest*, Issue 181, January/February 2013, p.24.
3) http://en.wikipedia.org/wiki/Seldom_Seen
4) http://en.wikipedia.org/wiki/Pony#Breeds_and_types_that_are_not_ponies
5) http://en.wikipedia.org/wiki/List_of_horse_breeds
6) Prystupa, et al. "Genetic diversity and admixture among Canadian, Mountain and Moorland and Nordic pony populations," *Animal*, The Animal Consortium, 2011, p. 1.

MONTY ROBERTS AND NATIVE PONIES

In 2007 Monty Roberts demonstrated his natural horsemanship techniques with a Dales Pony gelding. Mr. Roberts is best known for his join-up technique and his extraordinary success in training horses for many and diverse disciplines. Mr. Roberts had high praise for the British native pony breeds: "We've worked with most of the native breeds. I love them, and they're generally pretty easy, as they try to be cooperative." (1) His praise continued with regard to the Dales Pony gelding as a possible demonstration pony, "He's a nice pony. He's almost too nice! There's no problem with him, and the audiences wouldn't have believed that he's as raw as he really is." (2)

One of my ponies got similar feedback from Julie Goodnight, a natural horsemanship clinician in Colorado. Julie invited Lily to one of her demonstrations at the Rocky Mountain Horse Expo in 2004. The particular session was about starting to work with an equine, and unfortunately for Julie, Lily took everything in stride and was very responsive to everything Julie asked of her. There wasn't much to demonstrate! As Monty Roberts said, ponies try to be cooperative, which I've certainly found to be true.

(1) "Ellen's Dales and Monty Roberts," *The Native Pony*, December 07/January 08, page 36.
(2) Same as #1.

SHERLOCK HOLMES ON PONIES

A client shared with me the following excerpt from a Sherlock Holmes mystery she was reading. The veritable sleuth was in conversation with his colleague Dr. Watson, when Dr. Watson made a statement that Mr. Holmes felt he must refute.

"You endow the horse in your mind with more intellect than do the scientists, who place it well down the scale –"

"Your scientific colleagues may be right concerning the thoroughbred, Watson, but your Exmoor, Dartmoor or Fell Pony is a different creature, from a wild background where one slip … may mean death through falling from a crag or drowning in a bog. Anyway, I trusted Plodder (Exmoor pony) and he took me over the jumps, slowly and carefully – took nothing for granted."

My client said she was delighted to read Mr. Holmes's high opinion of ponies and that he called out Fells in particular. I couldn't help but smile for a different reason: the author chose to have his protagonist dive into the ongoing debate about the difference between horses and ponies!

GET MORE DETERMINED; PASS IT ON!

From the pony side of a partnership, we'll now shift to the person side. In much of the horsemanship I study, the human side of the horse-human relationship merits significant discussion. For instance, winter weather can often leave us feeling discouraged about our ability to make progress with our equines. To help us humans deal with these feelings, Horsemen's Jingle founder Jerry Williams suggests that sometimes it's better to invest a little time in ourselves because in the end we'll be better partners for our equines. He emphasizes that 80% of success is mental; it isn't always about 'doing.'

One night I got a phone call from a *Rural Heritage* magazine reader in response to an article I'd written. After getting briefly acquainted, we discussed the hard winter here and how he'd also been through some rough patches recently. He then shared a kernel of wisdom that had been passed on to him that helped him weather his storm: "Keep trying; don't get stuck because it makes you bitter." Wow. Sometimes simple words carry profound truth.

That phone call reminded me of another phone conversation around the same time. I had talked with my friend and mentor Joe, and I mentioned that our previous phone call had left me depressed. He had been tired and discouraged by a myriad of things related to breeding good horses and that fed into my own fatigue and state of mind. Joe acknowledged that things are challenging. He said, though, that he doesn't let himself get depressed. His kernel of wisdom was: "Don't get depressed; get more determined." Wow.

Both these kernels of wisdom are reminders that life presents us with lots of opportunities to make choices. We've all known bitter or depressed people, weighed down with regrets, unhappy at some level with choices they've made. These kernels are about making positive choices when less constructive ones feel natural and easier. Making positive choices is hard work but it is obviously a big part of success.

A friend once shared a perspective on depression that I'd never heard before: "Depression is not a sign of weakness, it is a sign that you have been trying to be strong for too long." It took me awhile to find the positive choice here, too. At first all I saw were questions: what if there's no choice about being strong? What if that's what circumstances require? The answers, of course, are that there are always choices; sometimes it can be tricky to find them, though.

Another friend gave me a book that helped me see the choice regarding being strong. *The Rhythm of Life* by Mathew Kelly identifies three key life practices: 1) adequate sleep, 2) an hour of quiet each day, and 3) one day totally off each week. So, regarding depression, taking some time off from being strong is the positive choice, even if it's just an hour a day, or a day a week. Wow.

These life practices actually weren't new to me, as similar practices are suggested by Julia Cameron in her *Artist's Way* work which I studied several years ago. Reminders are good, though, since life inevitably pulls me away from good practices. It's been really easy the last few years to fall into the trap of saying there isn't time for an hour of quiet a day, and it isn't possible to take Sundays off, even though I know that my life has more balance (or rhythm) when I make time for these life practices. Here's an applicable truism: "If you do what you've always done, you'll get what you've always got." Different choices are required if different outcomes are desired.

Several years ago a friend shared a quote about hope from Vaclav Havel. At the time I struggled with its validity. When the quote came around again though, it made much more sense. Havel said, "Hope is not a feeling. It is not the belief that things will turn out well, but the conviction that what we are doing makes sense, no matter how things turn out." I struggled with this quote when I first heard it because it made it sound like hope is a choice, not a natural state of mind. Now, though, it's much easier for me to see hope as something much more active than passive; it is indeed about choice. Wow.

Shortly after the phone call from the *Rural Heritage* reader, I focused on the kernel of wisdom about "Keep trying..." In hindsight, though, another important kernel emerged from that conversation. It was about 'passing on' words of encouragement and stories of renewed focus and reminders of wisdom heard once but forgotten. Sharing something that we've found insightful may be similarly valuable to someone else in our world. By sharing, we might give them an opportunity to have their own 'Wow' moment. In that spirit, I'm sharing these kernels in the hopes that you, too, will "pass it on!"

33

EQUINES, HUMANS, AND OXYMORONS

I got an email with a definition of the word 'oxymoron' that made me laugh. The standard definition, of course, is "a combination of contradictory or incongruous words." The email suggested that 'being sensible about horses' was an alternate definition of the word. The statement rang so true as to be humorous.

The following lines from Mary Lascelles poem "No Such Day as Sunday" come to mind:

> *'There's no such day as Sunday to laze around the fire.*
> *There's no holiday at Christmas with Shetland or a Shire.*
> *At Easter we're so busy with the sizes in between,*
> *And everyday there's feeding or keeping stables clean.*
> *To lie-in in the morning is something just unheard.*
> *And as for holidays abroad, that's something just absurd.*
> *We could jet our way around the world if we didn't have the horses.*
> *'You horsey people are quite mad,' I hear from many sources."* (1)

An article in *Horse Illustrated* magazine provides lots of evidence that involvement with horses is far from sensible. "State of the Equine Union: A Look at the Latest Trends in the Horse Industry" by Cynthia McFarland is based on a survey conducted by American Horse Publications in 2009-2010. For me, the most notable findings were:

- "the majority of participants owned the same number of horses as they did in 2007, before the recession hit." (2)
- "Almost three-quarters of surveyed horse owners said they were spending more money per horse than in 2007…" (3)
- "… more than 70 percent of horse owners surveyed said they would cut spending in other areas in order to make up for the extra cost of keeping their horses." (4)

In conversations about the small business that my husband and I jointly own, he will occasionally accuse me of being 'an engineer.' Usually it's when I make a very logical argument about a business situation, often based on financial information, while at the same time he sees non-financial reasons for coming to a different conclusion. It is true that I am an engineer by training, and I did learn to think about problems in very organized ways. And I have found, when it comes to my ponies, all that training means very little.

Logic says that if expenses increase, then reducing the number of horses to moderate expenses would be a sensible strategy. Obviously, logic isn't involved in horse ownership, since the survey found that people have the same number of horses and are paying more to keep them, reducing expenses in other places in order to maintain their horse herd. The same is definitely true for me.

The article also included the following statement that of course explains it all: 'Horse ownership is a lifestyle, not a fad." (5) We have horses in our lives for reasons other than logic or some passing whimsy. The nice thing about the *Horse Illustrated* article is that now we know that as horse owners we're not alone being the epitome of an oxymoron!

1) Lascelles, Mary. "No Such Day as Sunday," *Ponies and Dreams*, Creek Pony Collection, England, undated, p. 3. I highly recommend this book!
2) McFarland, Cynthia. "State of the Equine Union: A Look at the Latest Trends in the Horse Industry," *Horse Illustrated*, September 2011, p. 30.
3) McFarland, p. 31
4) McFarland, p. 31
5) McFarland, p. 35

TRAINING TIME IS ALL THE TIME

In 2011 I had the great good fortune to interview Doc Hammill for the first time. Doc is a nationally known horsemanship instructor with a special interest in draft and driving horses. The interview time flew by because we share so many interests and had so much to talk about. I was fascinated to hear him say the same thing that many of the other horsemanship instructors I've studied say: every moment we are with our equines, we are training them, whether we want to or not. Then he took it one step further, saying that he felt that all the time we spend with our equines outside formal training sessions actually has a bigger impact on the success we have with our hoofed friends than the formal training.

When I was picking up manure in the foaling shed around that time, my foal Madie was 'helping.' I could have just ignored her, but I've come to recognize an opportunity when it's presented to me. So I picked up each of her feet and asked her to yield her forequarters and hindquarters from each side. I also asked her to back up with a touch on the nose and then a touch on the chest. We also worked a little on boundaries, since I'm down at her level while doing the job and she explores how close she can get and with what part of her body.

Later in the day, I was giving yearling Libby her evening bucket of feed, and the dominant mare Ellie came to see if she could get in on the action. It's my responsibility of course to keep Ellie away from Libby and her bucket until Libby has finished her snack. Sometimes I just scratch Ellie in all her favorite places, but that day I decided to work on Ellie's yields. I asked her to back up by placing my hand on her nose and then her chest. And I asked her to step under herself both front and hind to disengage the forequarters and hindquarters. We worked on each one of these until we got good quality ones, and her reward was lots of praise and a good scratch on her withers.

The snatches of time I spent that day with Madie and Ellie can seem small and insignificant. Talking with Doc Hammill, though, reminded me that those sorts of sessions build toward a better working relationship down the road.

WORKING PONIES VS. DRAFT PONIES

Whether we are talking about Haflingers, Norwegian Fjords, Welsh Cobs, Shetlands, Welsh Ponies, Fell Ponies, or similar breeds, the working heritage of these ponies is diverse. The key element is that these animals were vital partners for their humans, whether it was packing hay or transporting trade goods, driving to market or to the doctor, pulling a sledge or plowing a field, shepherding for work or hunting for sport. Often the same animal was asked to do all of these jobs. Pony breeds are especially suited to this call to duty.

For a number of years I told people that my interest was in draft ponies. I realized, though, that I'd been misleading with that description. My interest is in working ponies in the broadest sense of the term, consistent with their heritage. I am interested in ponies that can be ridden, driven, packed, and worked in draft situations. This distinction was driven home when pictures of draft ponies were being shared on the internet.

Several years ago I was contacted by someone breeding draft ponies. When I did a little research, I discovered an organization dedicated to pony-sized versions of the big draft horse breeds (Percheron ponies, Clydesdale ponies, etc.) The pictures I saw on the internet were of these sorts of ponies. They were in a show ring on smaller versions of wagons that are traditionally pulled by the four- and six-horse hitches that are so popular at county fairs and expos.

As a pony enthusiast, I appreciate that people want to give ponies a chance to be in the public limelight like the big draft horses are. What sets ponies apart from draft horses, though, is their size. Before you laugh too hard at that statement, hear me out! The size of ponies enables them to be used for so many more things than the big draft horses and to do those things more economically. For instance, a pony named Samson works on a community-supported-agriculture (CSA) farm. Samson is used for more than field work, though. He is driven to town to deliver produce and he is ridden regularly. (1) I've had feet in both the draft horse and pony worlds for many years, and you're much more likely to see ponies put to multiple tasks than draft horses (or even riding horses).

Every one of us who have ponies have the opportunity to engage our ponies more than we do. It doesn't necessarily mean getting them going in harness, though that certainly expands the possibilities for 'more.' The point is that these ponies have historically been key contributors to their owners' lives, and it's been my experience that these ponies still want to have the broadest possible role with us that they can. It's up to us to figure out how to do that. Most of us don't live lives that are conducive to using our ponies in all of the historic roles: ride, drive, draft, pack. But with a little thought and creativity, we can engage our ponies in ways that will enhance their lives and ours, too.

Here are some ideas: If your mailbox is a hundred yards or more from the barn, why not use a pony for that short chore rather than a car or walking? How about picking up trash along a road? Desensitize your pony to plastic bags then take him or her for a walk carrying a garbage bag. Another possibility: it's likely that if you have a pony you're moving them between pasture and dry lot part of the year. Why not do that moving mounted rather than leading? Or how about ground drive instead of lead? Are you moving more than one pony at a time? Consider ponying one from the other. Or perhaps you walk through a dry lot to feed your pony. Consider riding your pony across that dry lot rather than transporting yourself on your own two feet. Do you have a wood lot and need to move fence rails but don't have your pony going in harness? Consider skidding the way I did when I first got started, from a mounted position.

And if working in harness is something within your sights, consider harrowing your arena rather than using a tractor or ATV. And of course there are myriad ways you can move manure with a pony in harness. I found when I got started that just spending time together with my pony gave me ideas for more things we could do together. All it takes is making it important.

Most ponies will appreciate getting to spend more time with you, and they'll appreciate that you thought to engage them differently doing odd chores. The new experience will likely enhance your relationship and make the regular things you do more enjoyable, too.

1)   "Samson makes the difference at Devon market garden," *Heavy Horse World*, Winter 2010, p. 66. With thanks to working pony enthusiast Eddie McDonough for pointing me to this article.

DON'T BUY A SKID STEER!

I'm kidding of course. Skid steers are very versatile machines. Ah, but there's that word 'versatile.' Just like a pony. So if you don't want to put your pony out of a job, or more accurately, if you want to keep your pony paying its own way, be very thoughtful if you're considering buying a skid steer.

As Christine Robinson pointed out, pones are the original ATVs. So it's even more important to give serious thought to an ATV purchase if you have a pony. Skid steers are a much better complement to a pony than an ATV. There are things a skid steer can do that a pony can't. I'm not sure you can say the same thing for an ATV.

Nonetheless, our skid steer did replace the ponies for some jobs in our business, most notably lifting things high and hauling brush. But in the complement department, a skid steer is handy when it comes to drilling post holes for fence, moving big bales of hay, raking brush, and moving pallets. And the skid steer has allowed me to have a bigger pony herd because of its role in manure management. Of course that touches on the idea of scale.

Keeping things such as manure management and hay storage at a level that can be handled without a machine has its advantages. There is something to be said for not paying five figures for something that will eventually wear out and isn't self-replicating like a pony can be. We could have bought some really nice horse-drawn equipment and hired some expert training assistance for an order of magnitude less money. And I can guarantee you I get a lot more enjoyment working my ponies than operating a machine.

There are numerous studies that document cost of ownership and profitability of horse-drawn versus machine-based operations. What is often not addressed is that once you go down the machine road, it's very hard to scale back. Most people who own a skid steer say they can't imagine how they ever got along without one. It's a question of scale and scope, how big your operation or business is and how diverse its activities are. Every situation is unique. For now, we're both-and: both a skid steer and ponies. I know which side I'll land on if we need to scale back!

WHAT'S POSSIBLE

I don't know where she was born or how she was bred or how she was initially trained. I can say, though, that my first pony taught me what ponies are capable of. The brand inspector called Mya the Wonder Pony a Shetland-Welsh cross when I bought her. Her 11.2hh size also suggests this breeding. Mya was my only equine for the first year. Because we lived in an isolated location, she was my frequent companion. She is still my closest equine friend.

Pat Burge found Mya for me. Pat coached me on what she knew was possible with a pony from her many years of partnering with them. That early coaching and Mya's equable temperament let Mya and I explore and experiment. We discovered together what was possible for us as partners, as you will read in the stories that follow.

Despite Mya's huge heart and willingness to work, I found for some things I needed more horsepower. As a two-year-old 13.3hh Norwegian Fjord gelding, Torrin came with the heritage and size to do work, but was only halter-broken. For the first year, Mya, Torrin, and I spent a lot of time together ponying, then I started Torrin in harness and doing ridden work. I'm thankful for the books *Training Workhorses, Training Teamsters* and *The Workhorse Handbook* both by Lynn Miller, as well as *The Fjordhorse Handbook* by Carol Rivoire. They all contributed to a start from which Torrin and I have never looked back, as you'll read in the stories to come. Torrin has done a lot of different things, but never as much as Mya. She's still the standard by which all other ponies are judged.

At the time that I went looking for a larger pony and found Torrin, Pat pointed me to the rare Fell Pony. Like Norwegian Fjord Horses, they are considered versatile. My interest was in using, but I ended up instead with breeding stock. Having these two breeds side-by-side has given me an incredible opportunity to learn about their different strengths and histories. They've also deepened my appreciation of working ponies immeasurably.

Another way in which Fell Ponies expanded my working pony education is introducing me to the world of British Native Ponies. Again I've learned about the different strengths and histories of these breeds. In addition, I've come to appreciate how the ways that they were put to use and their unique characteristics are intertwined with where they came from. I enjoy learning about the historic uses of all the breeds, and there's plenty yet to be discovered.

Partnering with ponies is a journey, not a destination. What my ponies and I do together will continue to evolve. Our journey will continue to be shaped by where we are located and the work that needs to be done. It will be shaped by each pony's unique characteristics. It will be shaped by what I learn that I can bring to the partnership. It's up to me to keep the journey going as we share life together.

The stories that follow are about the many things I've found possible to do with ponies. Many of the stories are about how I've involved the ponies in the work of the farm or the business. The variety of work we've done professionally has of course been made possible by how I interact with the ponies when we're not working, so there are stories here also about what's possible during off hours. I get almost as much enjoyment from that time together as I do working.

What I have found possible with ponies has to do with my particular partnership with them. You'll also read a story by Pat Burge about what she has found possible with one of her pony partners. May these stories about what's possible inspire you to discover what more is possible with your own partnered pony.

PAT'S STORY ABOUT MOONSHINE

MoonShine is a red roan pony with spots on his rump, under 14 hands. He is probably from the line of the Pony of the Americas breed that started with the little wild appaloosa stallion Dragon who evaded the Mexicans for years before they caught him. Moonshine is elegant with a very pretty face and perky ears that always listened for me.

MoonShine came to me through a kill buyer. He came with some negative issues of "I decide what we are doing," but came around to trust my ideas. Over the last 8 yrs. he has been an incredible partner on the trail, working with me on the Poudre Wilderness Horse Patrol in the Rawah Mountains of Colorado and Wyoming and breaking trail on U.S. Forest Service land and in ranch work during the winters at home. He has been on all kinds of wild terrain and has been courageous in jumping ravines and swimming. On one ride with a group of five, everyone reached a lake to take a drink, but Moon walked into the water and began to swim to the opposite shore! MoonShine has always been there for me; even if he lost me in rough country, he waited.

When we were out on the trail, Moon was very verbal. When tied to the trailer, he would wake me up very early in the morning with a series of nickers and whickers. Eventually, if I didn't respond, he repeated his series of pitched tones, and added a very loud whinny and then a very loud moan as the last proclamation. I would wait, fascinated to hear what else he would add to his own comments. Some sounds were long, some very short, and all were many different pitches! As a musician, I could not see how he was capable of this!

Moon became a victim of uveitis, a devastating eye disease. It's likely he was blind in one eye when he came to us, but we didn't know – he was just so willing and able. We had to remove one eye - all of us in the neighbor's garage, me holding Moon's head, Dick, and neighbor steadying his body, as our vet kneeled on a pad and proceeded to remove the eye over a grueling few hours. He was such an incredible patient, quiet and willing.

MoonShine has become blind in the last year and we have treated the disease for over a year, praying he could get some eyesight back. It is a huge loss for both of us. There has never been a depression, facing darkness coming over his days and nights. He is always optimistic, whinnies, comes up to me, nuzzles and nickers. He knows - two pellets for Moon - then the eye treatment in the eye - and then four more pellets for Moon! He has allowed me to be in the eye, numerous hours, days, weeks, months. He has taught me there is always a way.

He still takes me on some rough rides, and I verbally speak to him about the terrain. He does not spook but stops and looks at whatever forms he sees. He is still on the trail with me and does not want to retire yet!

He is the greatest trooper I have known and will always be my partner in every way, even in his up and coming retirement.

Here is a quote from Confucius that speaks of Moonshine's nature; he truly exudes this when I am with him. 'Where ever you go, go with all your heart.' And this quote from Ralph Waldo Emerson captures my partnership with Moon: 'Do not follow where the path may lead. Go, instead, where there is no path, and leave a trail.'

COURTESY WENDY FRANCISCO

How I Started Skidding

The picture here was taken about two months after I got Mya the Wonder Pony. It was long before I started studying natural horsemanship formally and also before I started working ponies in harness. Mya and I had graduated from a bridle and bit to a halter and reins, and we were using a bareback pad with stirrups that I'd borrowed from Pat. My intent in bringing Mya into my life was to get some help with chores. Yet I had no experience in working horses. In the end, that was a good thing, as I wasn't constrained by prior knowledge.

The fences on the ranch I was on were in need of repair. In particular, I needed to bring in some poles to finish enclosing the barnyard. Mya and I had already developed quite a rapport riding around the ranch, so I decided to see if she'd tolerate 'skidding' poles: I held one end in log tongs and we drug them along as we rode. It was no problem, and we moved a lot of poles this way. Eventually I found a work harness for her so that we could move more poles per trip and because my arm and shoulder and back were strained by the mechanics of the ridden approach. But our start skidding was ridden.

I got a phone call once from a Welsh Mountain Pony breeder who wanted to know how to get started with her four-footed friends. I talked her through what I was doing with Mya, and then I told her about some of the ways Mya and I got started. I shared with her about pony-powered garden carts, and I talked her through ground driving with a cotton rope harness. I had forgotten about 'ridden skidding' until I sent her some information on harness and implements. Then I started wondering if any pictures existed of how Mya and I started skidding. After some digging, some turned up. What memories they brought back!

Mya started me on a path with ponies, a path which has become dominated by Fell Ponies. The motto of the Fell Pony Society is 'You can't put a Fell to the wrong job.' Mya epitomizes for me the versatility of that motto, despite her Welsh-Shetland crossbred status. We have done so many unusual things together that I will always measure my Fells against Mya's accomplishments. As Christine Robinson wrote, ponies are the original ATVs/OHVs/quad bikes. Mya has helped me understand so many of the dimensions of that statement. I will be forever grateful for all she has taught me about using an 'original' ATV.

MOVING A RATTLESNAKE

Ridden skidding is unusual. Another unusual thing Mya and I once did came after we began harness work. I had bought a draft harness and collar at an auction, and without much effort we began skidding. Then I borrowed a cart from Pat, and we began driving. Looking back it all seems like it happened effortlessly. Mya certainly has spoiled me.

On the farm where we were living, I also kept ducks and had a goat dairy. We lived in rattlesnake country, though they weren't terribly common. One spring day, though, a rattlesnake appeared in the barnyard. It wasn't uncommon for me to have the goats loose in the barnyard when I was doing chores, and the ducks often were out all day, too, so having a poisonous snake in that space risked the safety of my animals. When one of the ducks stepped on the snake (fortunately the snake didn't react), I decided I needed to do something. Killing the snake seemed a bit extreme, so I decided I needed to move it. How to transport it became the next challenge.

I quickly settled on a solution. With a pitchfork, I lifted the snake and put it into a metal garbage can. It started rattling at that point, and the metal can made the noise more obvious. I harnessed Mya and hitched her to the cart and put the can in the cart next to me. We drove down the road a quarter mile and dumped the snake out, assuming that it would find a place to hang out where it wouldn't be disturbed.

Mya of course did this chore perfectly, and it was only in hindsight that I thought to appreciate her level-headedness. She wasn't bothered at all by the sound coming from the can on her cart, and she stood quietly and still when I disembarked the cart to empty the can's contents a short distance away. I never thought to question her ability to help with this chore. Now that I've had several other ponies in my life, I realize how lucky I am that Mya was my first.

HOLIDAY GREENS

For most of my life I have lived in forests. When I moved rurally, I started learning more about forest products and making a living from the woods. My first lesson in that regard was from a neighbor who made holiday greenery each year. He collected greens, cones, and bailing wire and made wreaths and garlands for clients. It was often a major endeavor for him to get the greens to his shed where he tied the wreaths, so one year I offered to help him. I hitched Mya to her garden cart, and we went into the woods where he had harvested his boughs and brought them out for him. It was a fun and festive event, with light snow on the ground and the aroma of fresh forest greenery adding to the occasion.

A few years later, I had moved and begun making my own holiday greens for sale. Naturally I involved my ponies. Because of my location, I used packs and pack saddles instead of a cart. Mya helped me bring in boughs several times, and each year a different Fell Pony helped bring in boughs or pine cones, too. My greens were shipped to recipients as far away as Iowa and, some went to New York City where they were resold in a garden store. I provided the shop owner with information on the use of pony power in the making of the greenery.

My wreath-making came to an end not because I lacked clients or help from ponies but because adequate greens became hard to find. Our forests were hit by an enormous epidemic that made life more difficult for forest inhabitants. I decided they needed the greens more than my clients did. Now I only occasionally make a wreath or garland, but you can be sure I involve the ponies in bringing in the supplies!

50

MOVING MANURE

Mya and I have been moving manure nearly since we started working in harness together. She just makes it so easy that it has taken me years to put anybody else on the job. She is always ready to go, whether it's been a few hours or a few months since we last worked in harness. She's always perfect, letting me use poor teamster habits like dropping the lines while I unload her cart. She stands without being tied or even without a halter at all while I harness and unharness.

In the lexicon of Parelli Natural Horsemanship, she is a Left-Brain Introvert (LBI), the perfect temperament for draft work. She has more whoa than go and tends to think rather than get emotional. An acquaintance described her similarly bred pony as being similarly tempered. As a likely Welsh-Shetland cross, Mya seems to have retained the work ethic of her long-ago forbears. Though the smallest pony here at 11.2hh, she is definitely the hardest worker of any of them.

Jerry Williams, 3 star Parelli Professional, has said that Left Brain horses are the most challenging. I can see that for people who want to 'go', an LBI like Mya would be frustrating. She's perfect for me because my goal for my life with my ponies is usually to slow the pace down. Most of my Fells, though, (and my Norwegian Fjord gelding) are Left-Brain Extroverts, still thinkers but more motivated to move. They are indeed more challenging to me because while they are compliant, they also need lots of mental stimulation which requires good leadership which for me requires lots of energy and planning which my whole life seems to need. Definitely a lesson for me here somewhere!

Mya is getting up in years, so it's time to get another pony going on manure duty. Because she's still so good at it, though, I keep putting the complete changing of the guard off. I'm thankful that I can go to Mya when something needs to get done and I don't have the energy to deal with the energy of the Extroverts around here. What a blessing this little pony has been to teach me what is possible with pony power.

MOVING FIREWOOD

When I moved rurally, I began heating with firewood. Bringing in enough firewood for winter was an obvious opportunity for the ponies to help. It was even more obvious because I'm not able to cut and chop firewood, so helping to move it was a great way for me to contribute.

The ponies and I have moved firewood using a variety of conveyances. Torrin and I began by moving firewood in a stone boat. I found the stone boat at Turkey Trot Springs where we lived after I got interested in working my ponies in harness. It was a sheet of aluminum attached to two 2x6 pieces of lumber, rounded up on the ends. It wasn't terribly sophisticated but it was light and worked well for the purpose. Mya and I have moved firewood with her adapted garden carts; she can move more with the aid of wheels than she can with a stone boat, so it's a better use of her energy.

Firewood can of course be moved by pickup truck or skid steer or other internal combustion conveyances. Moving firewood with ponies, though, is satisfying work in many ways and is always my preference.

MOVING WATER

For me, living rurally with ponies has always meant making the best use of the land resources available to keep my equine cost-of-ownership down. Sometimes that means using forage that has no source of water and is a long way from a well, so hauling water becomes necessary. In 2001 at Turkey Trot Springs, hauling water became necessary for another reason: drought. The creek dried up completely in one pasture I had fenced, so Mya and I hauled first a stock tank and then water to that pasture until the forage was gone.

After we moved to Willowtrail Farm, hauling water became a seasonal chore. During the months when freezing temperatures make above-ground water movement via hose more challenging,

hauling water to the farthest dry lot is necessary. Mya has always been a terrific help with this chore, as she'll stand still quietly while I dump the buckets into the stock tank.

There are indeed times when we use the skid steer for this chore, but it's always more fun and more economical to use a pony!

HERDING COWS

Trespassing cows was one of my original motivations for getting some equine assistance. I quickly learned after moving rurally that Colorado is a fence-them-out state, so it was my responsibility, if I didn't want the neighbors' cattle on my pastures, to maintain my fences and move the cattle off my land. Once again Mya spoiled me by being willing and able to move cattle. After I got Torrin I learned there really is something called cow sense; Mya had it and Torrin didn't. Torrin was much more inclined to turn the other way than to help me push cows back where they'd come from.

Usually my opportunities to herd cows are short, small, and local. Twice, though, I've been asked to use my ponies for short and small jobs elsewhere. One was to move some cows from one pasture to another to save a friend from having to do it by foot. The other was to move about 25 head off a pasture prior to a country wedding. My fondest memory of the pre-wedding herding was Mya facing down an Angus bull and getting him to go where we wanted. He was definitely bigger than she was! Torrin was more than happy to hang back and let Mya do the hard work. (Put a moose between Torrin and his hay, though, and Torrin will gladly move the intruder off!)

Herding cattle isn't something I do very often, and I've apparently always been more focused on the work than taking pictures. But it's sure nice to know that my ponies can help if necessary.

A Good Fit for Small Places

There have been a couple of jobs that our company has been asked to do where the ponies were an ideal fit. One place in particular allowed Mya's small size to really shine. The first year, the client asked us to rebuild a deck. The land was sloped and rocky and forested, and the deck re-building required us to excavate some soil prior to construction. The soil was dug out by hand, and our choices were to move it by wheelbarrow or have

Mya help. My preference was obvious. We parked Mya and her cart where it was convenient to throw soil, then when her cart was full, she backed it down and around a firewood stack and a tree before dumping it and bringing it back up to be refilled. She kept working without complaint through a rainstorm until the job was done. It's unlikely any piece of mechanical equipment could have accomplished what Mya accomplished that day, and it was certainly more fun for us working with her than a machine.

The next year the same client asked us to do some wildfire mitigation work. Mya's and my job was to move an old stack of firewood from near the cabin to a brush pile. Again Mya did most of the important work in reverse gear because the space was so tight that there wasn't room to turn around. She backed her cart over a bridge before dumping it and bringing it forward to be refilled. The bridge crossed a small irrigation ditch, and Mya never batted an eye about the work she was asked to do. She definitely earned her suffix 'the Wonder Pony' on this job. The hardest assignment turned out to be turning the horse trailer around when it was time to go home at the end of the day!

WILDFIRE MITIGATION

When the ponies and I moved to Gould, Colorado, we quickly got involved in my then-friend now-husband's logging business. The work where we contributed most was wildfire mitigation around cabins in the woods. Wildfires were headline news the first summer, and both Mya and Torrin went to work earning their keep.

Torrin mostly skid logs, while Mya mostly hauled brush. The logs were cut by a chainsaw, usually to 16' lengths. Torrin moved them to a deck where they were later removed by truck. Mya moved brush, either to the road where it was loaded into a truck and hauled off-site or to a brush pile. In either case, the brush was later burned during a winter snowstorm.

The landowners were thrilled to watch Mya and Torrin work. They appreciated the minimal impact of horse skidding, since the alternative was to use mechanical equipment. The ponies deftly avoided wildflower patches, rock flower beds, and sewer drain fields in their work. The only thing that really challenged them was a driveway with large cobbles. Moving the skid trail to the forest floor lengthened the route but enabled them to work barefoot more comfortably.

FENCE LINE CLEARING

A client asked our company to clear a quarter mile right-of-way for a fence. We didn't need to remove the wood, just get the downed timber out of the line of the fence. And oh, by the way, about 200 yards of the fence crossed a steep hillside. No problem for ponies!

We put a pack saddle on Mya so she could carry the lunch box, a chain saw (as far as the first tree), and miscellaneous other equipment. Torrin did the skidding.

It was a ten hour day by the time we finished, and we only took this one picture, at the beginning of the day when we were all fresh. At the end of the day, we were exhausted but also elated to have completed the project so efficiently. And I of course was thrilled that the ponies could participate.

BUILDING BUCK AND RAIL

One job where we have found the ponies especially helpful is building buck and rail fence for clients. Their involvement sometimes begins with skidding the rails out of the woods to a landing. Then once the rails are transported to the customer site, the ponies move the materials into the fence line.

Buck and rail tends to be the fence style of choice when terrain is rough, and the ponies shine there because they can often get the material into place on rough terrain more feasibly than equipment can. In situations of rough terrain, we often skid the buck materials and build them in place, then skid the rails into place, then assemble the fence.

Depending on the size of the pony involved and the terrain, we've also skid buck legs and rails together. It isn't necessary to have a particularly large pony for buck and rail work. The ponies seem to enjoy this sort of project because they can see a pattern and respond to it, such as skid a fence section into place then skid the next section to a logical next location.

Of course it isn't just rough terrain where the ponies shine on buck and rail projects. We've also built fence with the ponies' help when a client wanted ground disturbance minimized. This 'minimal ground disturbance' is a commonly cited advantage of horse logging and other natural horsepower applications.

LOADING AND LIFTING

Before we bought a skid steer, there were a couple of times when we needed to lift or load things that were too much for us humans. My husband devised ways that Torrin could help us.

One project where Torrin helped was a log barn. We had been using a two-person block-and-tackle system for most of the logs, but the long logs over the garage door were too much for us. Through use of cable and pulleys and risers, Torrin pulled the log up into place. The first picture shows Torrin waiting to be put to work, with the log in a starting position. In the second picture, you can see the log two-thirds of the way up the door; Torrin is holding it there while I took the picture!

It was easy for him, and it was definitely easy for us!

Later that same year, we were removing dying trees from around a cabin on a very small lot that was inaccessible by a log truck. My husband devised a ramp-and-chain system that allowed Torrin to load the logs onto our trailer. The bottom picture shows the ramp and chains, again with Torrin holding the load midway for picture taking! Such a good boy!

THE BRUSH PONY

While occasionally Mya has skid logs on jobs, more often she has specialized in brush work. On projects too numerous to count, she has tirelessly pulled her cart along forest trails while I collected brush, then together we headed for the nearest brush pile.

Usually our brush jobs proceeded peacefully and without much stress. There was one, though, that made me a little anxious. We were working in a quiet privately-owned forest. The owner had a large log home, and in the yard near the home, they had a life-size plastic deer as ornamentation. It was in the fall, which is mating season for large ungulates here, and the owners told us how many laughs they were getting watching a bull moose make amorous approaches to the plastic deer. Rather than finding it funny, my mind immediately imagined the bull moose wanting to get amorous with Mya! Fortunately, we only saw him once, at a distance, and he didn't seem to take much interest in us.

TIMBER CRUISING

In 2005, I was evaluating a timber sale on the ground ("cruising") in order to prepare a bid for our company. Because the sale was immediately adjacent to where we live, it was both feasible and convenient to do the cruising from pony back. Midnight, my seven year old stallion, was my partner, and we went out each day, riding through different units of the sale. I love riding ponies through timber because their smaller stature means I have to duck less under branches. Midnight was very accommodating, letting branches brush along his body, winding around trees, and stepping over downed logs, as well as patiently waiting when I needed to read a map to determine unit boundaries.

As is common when riding in the woods, there were several unplanned happenings on our rides. One day we got very wet when we were out in a snowstorm. Midnight was very tolerant. On a few other occasions Midnight decided to jump logs rather than step over them. At those times I was reminded that he could jump

two feet from a standstill without effort. I hadn't realized he could do it with me on-board as well! Fortunately, he didn't unseat me in this process. Leg aids were well-used for direction changes, as my hands were often busy pushing branches away from my face.

The day that we were out in the snowstorm, I lost track of my dog who always accompanied us. I called to her and continued our ride. A few moments later, Midnight indicated the direction from which Sadie was approaching. What appeared out of the trees in the snow, though, was not Sadie, but a rabbit that she was chasing, and it ran right under Midnight's nose, followed a short time later by Sadie herself. I felt blessed that Midnight just stood and watched the animal parade pass us by!

The picture shows me with an orange jacket on because it was hunting season. Another benefit of Midnight on these trips was his jet black color which was quite distinct from an elk or moose. Midnight was definitely a better mount for these trips than Torrin, whose coloring does resemble an elk!

On-the-Job Versatility Testing

I have read with interest the many articles about the evaluations performed by the Norwegian Fjord Horse Registry in which individual equines are graded against the breed standard. The stories about versatility are always what most interest me since that's what got me involved with working ponies in the first place.

Our company took on an unusual fence building project on public land in southern Wyoming that provided on-the-job versatility testing. We were to build buck-and-rail fence around mine openings to prevent snowmachiners and OHV users from inadvertently driving into them. A couple of people had been killed in the western U.S. when they drove their machines into open mine shafts.

Between the time we submitted our bid for the job and the time we were awarded the contract, winter set in, so we were working in snow. Two of the fence sites were in roadless areas, so my ponies were enlisted to help. Our bid using work ponies beat out a competing bid using the local high school football team!

The sites in the roadless areas were accessed by a bridge over the Encampment River. It was a metal arch about five feet wide and seventy-five feet long with wood planks. It creaked and groaned in the extreme cold weather that we faced. In addition, the frozen river underneath occasionally popped and cracked. I had never asked my ponies to cross a bridge like this, so I wasn't sure what to expect.

On one preparatory visit, I assessed how much of a challenge the bridge was going to be by taking Mya to it to see how she reacted. She also helped me assess trail conditions. Mya had no trouble with the bridge. Then we rode upstream on the trail towards one site. It was a magical ride, about twenty degrees Fahrenheit, winter sunshine, fresh snow, and just me, my favorite pony, and my dog. I was in ecstasy. There are definite benefits to this business!

Our job on that ride was to assess snow conditions and the possibility of skidding on the trail to one of the work sites. Mya and I found the trail snow-covered. Snow depths ranged from an inch to eighteen inches in places. And there was no way we were going to be skidding on it. Just after the bridge, the trail narrowed and on one side it dropped steeply to the river and on the other side it rose steeply up. It was also very rocky. That's when we knew we'd be packing material in.

So, on the next preparatory visit, we made sure the other ponies, Torrin and Sue, would cross the bridge. Neither of them had issues with the bridge either. I was still glad I had done a trial run on a friend's bridge and driveway that simulated what we faced in Wyoming. And I was grateful for how well all the ponies did traveling 2.5 hours each direction in the trailer. On one trip home, we encountered a blizzard, and I didn't

know that the high winds blew in one of the Plexiglas windows on the horse trailer. Thank goodness for mild-mannered ponies who endured the lower temperatures, increased ventilation, and pieces of plastic around their feet for the rest of the ride home.

The first project with pony content involved moving 32 16' rails and 12 6' buck legs about ¾ of a mile into the roadless area and up about 200 feet in elevation. The first section of ground to cover was from the parking lot across the bridge and to the base of a steep hill. Mya skid several of the poles and buck legs. Human power was used to get the rails and buck legs up the steep hill as well as along the last 200' to the mine opening.

In between, the ponies needed to skid uphill about 5/8 of a mile through snowdrifts and sage and rock (fortunately the snow had buried the cactus). Mya made about 10 round trips over two days and Torrin made 8 trips in one day. Below is a picture of this crew at the start of the trail; the end of the trail is the tree in front of my nose in the far distance. The trail however took us up and around due to two intervening rocky gullies. It was tough, tiring work, and these two ponies definitely proved their mettle.

The second project with pony content involved moving 12 6' poles and 4 6' buck legs two miles into a wilderness study area. Three ponies were required for this much material. Neither Torrin nor Sue had ever packed before, yet they did well on their first outing with awkward loads and tough ground conditions.

To make matters even more interesting, on the day of the pack trip there was a freshly killed deer (probably by coyote, possibly mountain lion) right along the trail at the start. The ponies didn't even pause when they smelled and saw it. I'd been told that the smell of blood usually bothers equines, so no reaction was a good one! At right is a picture of my packing ponies at the end of the trail.

We had one employee assisting us with this project. He had no equine experience, so on the packing trip, we gave him Mya to lead. He said she was just like leading a dog, very easy! Thank you, Mya!

There was one day when things didn't go as planned. We'd hoped to use Torrin and Sue, the two larger ponies, to work as a team to do the uphill skidding. The day we tried it, the wind was howling, and the starting point of the skid was very exposed. Sue made it very clear she had no interest in working in those conditions. For the safety of all concerned, we changed plans and had Mya and Torrin do the skidding on a different, calmer, day. Overall, though, the pony projects were successfully completed, and I was very pleased with how well my pony partners did. Pony versatility was proved to me on these projects, without the need for a society-sanctioned evaluation!

OUTSTANDING PERFORMANCES

On another unusual job, three ponies helped us again. The job involved a ninety minute one-way trailer ride, a quarter mile walk into two cabins, and the felling, skidding and piling of over one hundred dead lodgepole pine trees. The cabins sat on the edge of the very picturesque Big Creek Lake, and Lily, my seven-year-old mare was the first pony out of the trailer. Once tied to a tree, her attention was immediately drawn to the body of water below her. She'd seen rivers and creeks and ponds before but never a lake the size of this one. It was fascinating to watch her take in the motorboats and fishing folk and the generally impressive scene.

Lily's job was to pack in miscellaneous tack and equipment for the day's work. Torrin was slated to skid the

larger logs that we hadn't hand-piled previously. Mya had her usual brush job, pulling her cart loaded with debris to brush piles.

On the days when we'd been preparing for the ponies' arrival, the weather had been sunny and hot. This day was completely different, with clouds, cooler temperatures, and three intense thundershowers, one of which dumped marble-sized hail for a few minutes while I had Mya hitched. I was very impressed that all three ponies stoically endured.

The greatest challenge of the day for me, though, was the trail in and out. After unloading and tying the ponies to trees at the trailhead, Mya and I rode the trail (bareback with halter and leadrope as usual) so she would know what was ahead of her. It was a short but incredible ride, along the edge of the lake, just my pony, my dog, and me. Our next venture down the trail was quite different, as Mya pulled her metal cart, and I helped ease it over boulders the size of ice chests. It was a noisy trip, despite the rubber wheels. I was amazed that the glass jars in my vet box survived the ride in the cart. Lily impressed me greatly as she followed me with her packs, her lead rope slack, so I could drive Mya and help her avoid the smaller obstacles in the trail.

Once on-site, Mya had the most work, hauling brush. Torrin accomplished his skidding in about an hour because my husband's forty years of logging enables him to set up skids very efficiently. When Torrin finished, we wished we'd left more for him to do and not hand-stacked so much ourselves! When not working, the ponies were tied out in a grassy area away from where trees were falling.

Our clients arrived a few hours after we did, but they didn't tell us until later that they were expecting ten more people at sundown. I was thankful for my mild-mannered ponies because they didn't give the new arrivals much thought as we departed.

Our trip out at dusk was as uneventful (and noisy) as our trip in had been, which is what made the ponies' performances so outstanding. They seemed to appreciate the opportunity to contribute, each in their unique way, to a job well done, ending the day peacefully eating hay while we cooked our own dinner before heading home. As we loaded the ponies after dark, just as lightning began to crack again nearby, I was immensely thankful for being able to share my working life with these ponies. The picture of Lily at the trail head above the lake is the only one I took that day because I had my hands full with the work at hand and three ponies to tend to.

PRE-GRAZING FOR TURKEYS

Many years ago I learned about the use of grazing animals to restore and sustain landscapes. Many landscapes evolved ecologically with native grazing pressure as part of their existence. In some cases, modern implementations of conservation grazing attempt to mimic that native grazing.

More recently I've learned of conservation grazing using British native ponies. In places the ponies are improving habitat for endangered butterflies, in others for endangered wildflowers, and in others they are helping to control non-native species.

My modest implementation of intentional grazing had to do with turkeys. As you can see in the photograph here, our hay meadows grow grass quickly, thickly, and tall. I was raising a heritage breed of turkey called Blue Slates, and I had them in moveable pens so they could graze and eat insects. Unfortunately, the grass in the pasture was too tall by the time the turkeys were ready to go out in their pen, so I needed to shorten the grass. My solution was to pre-graze the grass with ponies. You can see in the picture that I focused the ponies' grazing by putting up portable panels. They would graze the grass to about 4-6" in a few hours then I would take them home, and the turkeys were able to enjoy grass of a height that worked for them. I had to concentrate the ponies' grazing activity to get the result I wanted; they would normally take months to get the grass to a turkey-acceptable height where I needed it. So the turkeys benefited from the ponies' activity, but the ponies benefited from the turkeys' activity, too. The next year, the areas where the turkey pens had been were noticeably greener and more lush from the manure the turkeys left behind. A win for the turkeys, a win for the ponies, and a win for me using the pasture grass effectively!

MYA'S BIG SPOOK

A friend shared a story about her pony spooking while driving down a familiar road because something unusual happened. It made me think about one time that I had something similar happen with Mya. It's the only time she's ever spooked at anything while working (in training sessions she's made her opinion known about sleigh bells and plastic bags on her body – not interested, thank you very much).

We'd been working in harness for a few years and were skidding fence posts at a client's site, something we'd done hundreds if not thousands of times before. We were about one hundred fifty from their house, skidding towards the house when the client's son came out of the house wearing a cape.

He started running down the hill towards us, and the cape started billowing out, and he may have been yelling. Mya tried to do an about-face, which is NOT a good thing when attached to a log. Fortunately I got her calmed down, and the son got yelled at by the mother.

All's well that ends well.

AN ADVANCE IN WORKING MYA

By now you know that Mya the Wonder Pony is the equine who has set the standards for me as the ultimate working partner. We've herded cows, packed chainsaws, skid logs, placed in a driving show, ridden solo in all manner of places, and hauled a number of unusual things, including rattlesnakes needing relocation. Several years ago I had a horsemanship instructor challenge me to advance my relationship with Mya. While idealistically I could see his point, practically I didn't see any reason. Though Mya does draw the line at carrying plastic bags and sleigh bells, she's so good at everything else that finding things to improve felt like making unnecessary work for myself.

However, I did finally decide to work on one small part of our relationship: bridling. Torrin was the motivation for this work. Whenever I go to put his work bridle on, he reaches enthusiastically for the bit. In this he has set the standard, not Mya. Putting the bit in her mouth, by contrast, has always been a matter of inserting my thumb in the corner of her mouth to encourage her to open up. I never liked this approach because it felt a little like forcing the bit in her mouth, though she never fought me. So eventually I worked with Mya to the point that she would take the bit into her mouth when it was presented. It

wasn't a quick process, as during each session she took her own sweet time deciding that she was willing. Nonetheless, having her open her mouth when the bit was offered rather than me forcing her mouth open to insert it was an advance in our bridling relationship.

Because of an injury to Mya (she got kicked in the head), we had a break in our work routine for a couple of months. When we started back up, I was pleased to discover that we'd made another advance in our bridling relationship. She actually reached for the bit. I was amazed. She's still not as enthusiastic as Torrin is, but after nearly thirteen years, it was really something to experience this offer on her part.

When these ponies reach for the bit, when they ask to have a piece of metal inserted in their mouth, it's really quite an extraordinary thing if you stop to think about it. It would take quite a bit of convincing for me to let someone insert metal into my mouth! When they reach for the bit, I can't interpret it any other way than they want to go to work with me. There's no force or coercion or reward system involved here. They are offering of their own free will. In the business that my husband and I own, we've had human employees who weren't as interested in working as these ponies are, and they were getting paid! It's stunning when I stop to ponder it.

When I think back to this advance in bridling Mya, I recognized there was a sudden change in our bridling relationship after a break of two months, from her taking the bit to her reaching for it. It felt to me like she'd missed working together. For me this change was more than just an indication of improved horsemanship on my part. It felt like a statement by Mya about our partnership. She was twenty, and she still wanted to work with me. How cool is that?

FESTIVE FUN WITH PONIES

Just as I've tried to integrate my ponies into my work life, I've also tried to involve them in other aspects of my life, too. Three ponies, for instance, "stood up for me" at my wedding. Torrin wore his work harness and even did a short demo before the ceremony for one of the guests. Mya had a foal at foot who wandered about outside the ring of people, and Lily represented the Fell Pony herd as my first-born.

The winter holiday season has been the most impacted by having ponies because I no longer travel to be with my human family. Instead I have tried to involve the ponies in my festivities. One year on Christmas Eve, my husband and I rode into a nearby subdivision to deliver cookies to anyone at home. The next year we put Mya and Torrin to carts and drove with guests to do the same festive errand. While Mya wanted nothing to do with the sleigh bells I have, Torrin kindly obliged to wear them.

More recently, we've taken to staying right at home for the holidays. The current tradition is to wassail the ponies, feeding them apples and wishing them good health for the coming year.

I also send out a photo greeting at the holidays; the photo is taken of pony ears, with a caption that says it all: "May Your New Year Be Filled with Lots of Time in the Best Place: Behind a Pair of Pony Ears!"

PROBLEM SOLVING PONY-STYLE

While I originally brought ponies into my life for work, I now find that I get satisfaction from time we spend together when we're not working. This story is about one of those times.

I lease summer pasture about four miles from home. One day when I got to pasture to pick up Mya, Torrin, and Lily to bring them home, I was presented with two problems. I solved them with pony assistance and was quite pleased with myself!

First, Mya was in the same spot she'd been in the two previous days when I'd arrived at pasture. Between her location and mine was a pool of irrigation water which meant I had to take off my work boots and don irrigation boots in order to halter her and load her in the trailer. Then I had to reverse the footwear process. Except if I tried to solve this problem pony-style. For some reason, I finally had the good sense to do that!

I had the brilliant idea to ride Torrin over to where Mya was and then pony one of them back. Torrin could have wet feet, and it would save me time since I had to halter Torrin anyway (and he has the good grace to come to me when I show up.) Plus it was fun to ride Torrin for the first time in a while. Mya didn't seem too thrilled with this solution since I did indeed get there more quickly, and her preference was to stay on green grass as long as possible.

The second problem was presented by strong winds that were blowing the trailer door shut as I was trying to load the ponies. For Mya, I was able to hold the door ajar and send her under my arm into the trailer. I then followed, tying her and closing the divider. Torrin was the second to be loaded, but he's too big to go under my arm, so I loaded him from the off-side, tossing the lead rope on his back as he went in, then I followed him to tie him in place. The wind grew even stronger as I was tying Torrin, and the door was just ajar enough for Lily to stick her head in to check my progress. That gave me the idea for loading her. I hadn't haltered her yet, but she was awfully good at liberty, so I held the door open wide and suggested that she load herself. In true pony style, she made no move but was thinking about it, so I gave her further encouragement, and she hopped into her place. I shut the door behind her, then fetched the halter and went into the trailer to halter her and tie her in place.

At the time I was reading *The Soul of the Horse* by Joe Camp. Camp stresses that equines offer us relationships that have depth and quality if we will only accept them. It was a thrill to find that my relationships with these ponies had sufficient quality to solve some small problems with their assistance, pony-style!

PONYING AFTER DARK

The last thing I wanted to hear at 9pm at night was galloping hoofbeats coming up the drive. I was outside giving my ponies their last feeding for the day, and I was really looking forward to going to bed. I knew that galloping hoofbeats could only mean more work to do, and I wasn't thrilled. In a few moments, the three ponies I expected to see – Mya, Torrin, and Lily – came into view. I knew their destination: the haystack at the house. Everyone else had been fed, and my three culprits were tired of waiting while I finished my other chores before feeding them.

My three culprits were housed in a one-acre pen enclosed by a single strand of electric fence. I had not had the fence electrified because I was charging the battery. Lily knows when the fence is off, and she sometimes plays with the gate. The last time I'd seen these three unannounced like this was due to Lily's ingenuity. Another time, I'd seen them unannounced when a moose took the fence out.

I haltered my three friends and considered the couple-hundred-yard walk to their paddock. It didn't take much pondering before I jumped on Mya's back and started ponying the other two back to their paddock. I'd been ponying these three this way for several years, but I hadn't ever done it after dark. They were all quite animated after their escape. Mya tends to break into a trot to stay ahead of Torrin who walks faster than she does. Lily then follows suit then Torrin. So I was engaged for the ride down the driveway trying to keep everyone at a slow gait. We all made it without being too peeved at each other.

I got everybody tied then started investigating why the fence was down. As near as we could determine, the extreme cold of the previous few days had taken a toll on one of the ceramic insulators. It had broken, causing the fence to pop free and the gate to fall down. That's all it would take for these three to investigate what the rest of the herd was eating.

I take as a small reward for delaying my bed time the thrill of ponying these three. I often get a thrill when I'm working with just one pony, and working with three like this heightens the experience. I'm just glad moose damage wasn't the cause of the adventures of the evening, as ponying these three and seeing a moose while doing it would have been more excitement than I needed at 9pm!

THE BLUE TARP

When we're not working. I often call what we do playing games; others might call it ground training. This story about a blue tarp provides an example.

I went out one afternoon to play with my stallion Apollo, taking with me a brand new blue plastic tarp. I didn't know what to expect, as plastic is unpredictable with my ponies. Mya, who rarely is bothered by anything, takes exception when it comes to plastic. Willow, in contrast, at a year old learned to play around the world (meaning stand still while I stroked him with a plastic bag at the end of a stick) in a quick five

minute session. With Apollo, I found that the $5 I spent on the tarp was the best entertainment money I'd spent in a long time.

Apollo had been begging for attention, and I'd been obliging him every day. He was at an age when variety was important, so I decided to see if he would walk over a blue plastic tarp. It was about five degrees above zero with little sun, so the plastic of the tarp's wrapper crinkled loudly in the sharp cold air. I set the tarp down outside his pen, and he immediately came over to investigate. I went in and played with him at liberty and then with a halter and lead rope then decided to get started with the tarp.

As I handled the bag in front of him, he seemed more interested and curious than concerned, only taking a half step back when I tore the bag open. I put the tarp on the ground and took the bag to the edge of his paddock. Apollo was already pawing at the folded tarp on the ground in my brief absence. I unfolded the tarp to a 3'x8' rectangle with his help, and the tarp slithered easily over the freshly packed snow. I moved the tarp by sliding it, and Apollo followed along, clearly very interested. I realized I didn't need to encourage him to explore it, so I stepped back, holding the lead rope. He pawed it, sniffed it, and then started trying to bite it. When he lifted it for the first time, he was surprised and dropped it, but immediately went back for more. The next time he got it in his mouth, he tossed it into the air, which surprised him and he dropped it and stepped back. Then he got it in his mouth and tossed it again, this time not letting go. It draped over the lead rope and so kept following him as he moved away, which unnerved him until I managed to shake the tarp off the rope. Then I undid his lead rope to give him full freedom to experiment.

I wish I had had a video camera. It would definitely have caught my laughter, and the sheer joy that Apollo had biting, pawing, and tossing the tarp. Towards the end he pawed it up under his belly and stood still with it there, as if contemplating what he had done and what to do next. He picked it up and pulled it with him as he backed away. He lifted it from underneath and tossed it. After a second performance of pawing it into a pile under his belly, he came to me, as if finished with his exploration.

I took the opportunity to reattach his leadrope to his halter and straighten the tarp on the ground. I then asked Apollo to walk over the tarp, which ended up being anticlimactic, as he had already desensitized himself to it. He walked straight across in one direction and only slightly hesitated in the opposite direction. I shook my head as I thanked him for the entertainment.

SOME SPONTANEOUS PLAY

It all started when I went to get my mare Lily. I was short of ideas on how to make our session interesting for her. I've found that if I can surprise her with something new and fun to do, she's much more willing to engage in my training agenda. But when I got to the gate, I still hadn't had any inspiration. Fortunately, just being around my ponies often provides what I can't find alone, and sure enough, within a few minutes of being with Lily, we were trying something new and unusual.

As we left her paddock, I threw the lead rope over her neck and asked her to follow me at liberty. We had been doing this often. It was a fairly 'safe' test of our partnership, as there was deep snow everywhere, so she wasn't likely to wander off to find something to eat (though one day she did detour to flirt with my stallion.) This time she stayed right with me, trotting when I did, stopping when I did. Then I added a new twist. When we were stopped, I lowered my head to the ground. She tried a few things to see if they were what I wanted, then I pulled down on the lead rope. After her head came down to my level, I raised up and asked her head to follow mine, rewarding her when it did. After about five repetitions, she got the idea without a hint from the lead rope. It was cool! We tested it about half an hour later on our return to her paddock. At first she didn't follow me, but then she remembered, and down came her head. Cool again!

When we got back to her paddock, Mya and Torrin were in high spirits trotting around because the weather was changing. After I released Lily, Torrin trotted by, so I started trotting after him. Mya then followed me. The three of us did one circuit, after which I'd had enough jogging on soft snow. Torrin completed his second circuit and came to me, happy to have played along. Very fun. I hadn't had time to play with Mya and Torrin much, so we all really appreciated this short spontaneous game.

Pat's pony Tugboat was the first pony I ever ground-drove. After getting Mya, it quickly became apparent that harness work was possible. At an auction, Pat helped me pick out a harness and collar. We took it back to Lost Creek Ranch and put it on Tug so I would know how to fit it to Mya when I got home. The harness was much too big for Tug, but he went along with training me anyway.

It was my first lesson in the necessity of adapting things for working with ponies. Ponies come in all shapes and sizes. Mya's work cart is too small for Torrin, and Torrin's work sled is too heavy for Mya. As much of a challenge is the fact that ponies are a different scale than most horses. Ingenuity is therefore required to get things done. I've adapted stone boats, sleds, carts, pack saddles, harness, singletrees, and skidding chains. I've started collecting information on riding saddles; there are more pony-friendly options now than ever before. In general, there is much more pony-sized equipment available than there was when I got started. My garden and ATV cart modifications that you will read about were key enablers of work. I've also included an article on harness and one on round pens. There is obviously a lot more that could be written about adapting things for working with ponies. I have written a number of articles on harness for *Rural Heritage* magazine that are available in back issues and will eventually be published in book form.

As I reflect on all the practical topics about pony-person partnerships, it's clear there is a spectrum, from things that are applicable mostly on the person end to things that are mostly on the pony end. On the person end, I've included stories about organizing the day, a helpful form of coaching, and a real life lesson in making lemonade out of lemons. On the pony end, there are several stories about ponies and their herd dynamics that can inform our relationship with them. In between, where ponies and people interact more closely, there are stories on basic handling and matching a pony to their work. These practical considerations all help maximize our ponies' <u>desire</u> to partner with us.

Then there are stories about maximizing our ponies' <u>abilities</u> to partner with us. When I met Pat and Dick, Commanche was Tug's sidekick. Commanche is a Shetland stallion and was my first introduction to pony breeding stock. Pat shared the various tricks she used when Commanche needed to serve a mare that was bigger than he was. For many years Commanche's stud fees paid for the feed for the pony herd, even though he got very little of the feed himself. It was at Lost Creek Ranch that I learned that not only did every equine get a custom ration, but that that ration varied in size, in content, and that it varied over time and sometimes within a particular day. You will read several stories about the feed choices I've made.

Because I live a long way from anywhere, I have learned to be the first responder for any health issue that my ponies present. To minimize my stress and maximize my chances for success, I have chosen to take a very proactive and preventive nutritional approach to the health of my herd. I was fortunate to be introduced to a line of products which are particularly well suited to my situation. I've included a few stories about being a first responder for my ponies. There are many more stories on my website. There also a few stories about other healing practices I use to keep my ponies healthy.
As I mentioned in the introduction, I believe proper hoof care is crucial to a pony's ability to perform at their highest level. Part of my early education at Lost Creek Ranch was about hoof trimming, thanks to Pat's husband Dick Vessel. You'll read several stories about what I've learned since those early lessons with Dick.

One of the things that can be appealing about using real horsepower to do work is the ability of equines to reproduce themselves. I have collected what I have learned about breeding ponies in my book *Fell Ponies: Observations on the Breed, the Breed Standard, and Breeding.*

Pat's story about Tugboat leads things off in this section about what is practical. I am grateful that I knew him and for the lessons he patiently taught me about partnering with a pony.

PAT'S STORY ABOUT TUGBOAT

Tugboat was a stocky little eleven hand tank. He was ill-cared for before, so we worked through the laminitis and Cushings disease.

Tug was to be my wheel chair after hip surgeries. He not only was that, but he became my everything. Housed outside my bedroom window, Tugboat carried me down the hill to lead horses to pasture from corrals, then back up to the house carrying groceries and full milk jugs for the week - and me. He was indispensable in so many ways.

When the holidays came, Tugboat carried me to the woods in his little work harness, and as Dick trimmed small blowdown trees, they were tied to Tugboat and down the mountain he came with glee, making trees fly in the air, and giving me a ride to remember! A stop at the barn, and then up the hill to the house. He loved to do this, especially with his buddy, littler Commanche, who also delighted in doing anything Tug could do.

From riding fence to swimming me over a river - Tug could do it all! Little Tugboat passed on in incredible physical and mental shape - the last month he could still run a mustang out of his favorite barn! The vets aged him at 40 or more! We sure wish we could tell the universe to bring him back.

PONY-POWERED GARDEN AND ATV CARTS

Having the ability to move things with my ponies has been a key enabler in partnering with them on and off the farm. Here are two pictorial descriptions of modifications I've had made to first a garden cart and second an ATV cart. For Mya, the ATV cart is just the right size; the garden cart was a bit small.

> **Caveat**: You'll notice that these modified carts don't have a true singletree. They definitely need one, and I have added one to the modified ATV cart that I use now. You either need to add a true singletree to these designs or at least put rubber straps between the hooks on the carts and the harness heel chains to allow for some give to minimize the chance of injury to the pony's shoulders.

The Modified Garden Cart

As a child, I spent a lot of weekend days helping my parents in the yard, imagining myself as a pony pulling the garden cart. Perhaps that is what led me to work with my first husband to modify our garden cart for Mya. We took a standard garden cart, available from most garden supply stores, and added shafts and a single tree (the pony kit). The width of the cart needs to match the width of the pony so that you don't have to make too many modifications for shaft width. Garden carts come in a variety of sizes so finding one to match any small pony should be possible.

Our design was for hauling loads with the teamster walking alongside or behind the load. There are modifications that put a seat on top of the cart and use the cart primarily for riding. Most garden cart construction though isn't stout enough for that use.

We wanted our modification to the garden cart to be relatively easy to remove so a human could still be the draft animal. One problem arose, though, with the front stand that is fixed in place. We found that the stand often caught on bumps in the terrain. This created significant jarring on the whole system and caused the pony a bit of consternation as well. One bump actually broke our first set of shafts that were made out of cottonwood poles. We tried tilting the stand up, but we found that unless the stand is screwed in place it easily falls down. We finally decided to remove the stand and dedicate the cart for pony use. The pony kit can still be easily removed and the stand put back on for human-draft use.

We ended up using 2"x4" lumber for the shafts. We did some carving of the front ends to improve the interface with the harness.

As you can see from this photo taken from the rear, the fundamental design has four cross pieces connected across the shafts. The purpose of the rear cross-piece is to provide a bit of a push for the cart. The forward movement of the cart is provided in part by the forward-most cross-piece. The cross-piece just forward of the rear, mounted on top is what keeps the pony kit from dropping down onto the tires. It should be placed just far enough forward to allow the rear gate on the cart to easily slide up and down. The cross-piece third from the rear is placed slightly forward of the front of the cart body and below the handle. It helps to lift the handle and, more importantly, it pushes the cart back when reversing. The front cross-piece is also the single-tree (see the next photo for more detail). Two fairly heavy hooks set into the 2"x4" cross-piece accept the heel chains; again for the safety and comfort of the pony, a true singletree should be used or rubber straps put between hooks and heel chains.

The blocking behind the handle helps to pull the handle (and the cart). The blocking on top of the handle pivots to cover the handle and keep it from rising up.

It is easy to remove the pony kit from the cart, though it can be a bit of a puzzle the first time. You have to swivel the blocking on top of the handle to free the handle. Allow the shafts to drop while you lift the cart handle. You then lift the rear of the pony kit above the back of the cart and pull the cart back from within the pony kit.

Since we had not worked Mya in shafts much, other than in a travois configuration, we decided it was best to try her out in the pony kit without the cart. It turns out that it can indeed function as a travois.

One of the most common uses of the cart was to haul and spread manure on the pastures. It was also used to haul bales of hay, firewood, t-posts, a dog house and a collection of wooden posts. I retired the garden cart when I got an ATV cart that my husband Don modified.

The Modified ATV Cart

Several factors suggested a different working cart solution:

1)	I found the garden cart too small for many applications;
2)	The garden cart couldn't be dumped; and
3)	Mya could handle larger loads than the cart could.

The next step then was to experiment with a small ATV dump cart. The garden cart required wood-working skills. The ATV cart requires metal-working skills.

We removed the ball from the store-bought 17 cu. ft. ATV cart, leaving a flat tongue, onto which we bolted a triangle of flat steel.

To the front of the steel triangle we welded a piece of angle iron that was as long as the shafts are wide. We then affixed a set of steel shafts that we had on hand to the angle iron. The hooks on the shafts that can accept the heel chains are underneath the angle iron and not visible in the photos.

Note: *a true singletree should be added to this design for the comfort, working effectiveness, and safety of the pony.*

While this cart can dump, it doesn't dump very well. I next hope to find or build a larger cart for my larger ponies that will completely dump its load.

NORWEGIAN HARNESS

I decided to try Norwegian harness because of the Norwegians' long history of working ponies. I figured they had a better chance than most at getting some of the harnessing challenges right.

One of the features of the harness is integrated hames and collar with lots of adjustments. This enables me to modify the fit as my pony's neck changes shape due to weight gain or loss, winter or summer coat, in working shape or out of shape. I don't have to buy different collars for different parts of the year.

Another feature has to do with the angle of draft. I feel the angle of draft is especially crucial to consider when working ponies because I want to maximize efficiency to get the most out of my small equines. The Norwegian Harness, like the D-ring harness from New England, attaches the traces not to the hames but to a ring that is held at the appropriate angle relative to the collar. It is possible to make adjustments to the more common Western brichen harness to achieve the same ideal angle of draft.

Another feature of Norwegian harness is common to driving harness but not often to draft: the crupper. I've always been uncomfortable with the idea of wrapping a harness piece around the base of the tail, but I've gotten over that. A crupper provides so much security, keeping the harness from slopping from one side to another, which I've seen happen numerous times with my conventional Western brichen harness.

The backpad of my Norwegian harness also has significant padding, which I think is important for comfort. I heard a story once of someone putting a horse in shafts without adequate padding under the backpad and ending up with bad sores there. Padding just makes sense under the backpad. It's one of the first additions I made to my Western brichen harness when I started working ponies.

Two other features of the Norwegian harness I haven't put to use yet. For working between shafts, the Norwegian harness is designed for the attachment point to be at the ring rather than at the end of the traces. Unfortunately this requires customizing shafts on my carts, which I haven't gotten to yet. The Norwegian harness also has a second belly band to act as additional braking against the back of the front legs. Again, since I haven't hitched to carts, I haven't been able to evaluate this feature.

Over all I've been pleased with my Norwegian harness. I have definitely had to make customizations here and there to use it in my situation, but it's been worth the effort so far.

ROUND PEN SYTLES AND CONFIGURATIONS

I've been asked more than once about round pens. I know some horse trainers swear by them, and others don't think they're necessary. I am on my second round pen, and our company has built a round pen for a client; all three are different styles. I didn't need a round pen when I got my first pony, but now that I keep stallions, raise youngstock, and train for riding and driving, I couldn't be without one. That being said, I wouldn't want one other than the style I currently have, for many reasons.

Here is a description of a round pen from the novel *Boleto* by Alyson Hagy that is completely different from what I have.

"The round pen was as secure as a fort, which was what he and Chad and Everett had used it for when they played cavalry soldiers and Indians as kids. He was too young to remember his father building the pen, but he knew his father had done it, as he did so many other things, the right way. The peeled logs that made up the fencing were no more than six inches in diameter, and each of them had been sunk into the ground to a depth of at least six feet. No coyote would ever be able to dig its way into the pen. And no unmannered mustang would ever be able to break its way out. The fence was every bit of six feet tall. The pen was thirty feet in diameter." (1)

When I first bought a pony, I began studying fencing. I quickly learned to think in terms of the types of barriers a fence provides. A physical barrier is one that is strong enough to withstand bodily pressure; wooden fencing is usually a physical barrier. A psychological barrier is one that makes an animal think they are confined; a good example is a single strand of electric fence to which the animal is trained. Another example of a psychological barrier, in my climate, is deep snow. The final type of fence is a visual barrier; an example of a visual barrier fence is woven wire; it gives the appearance of being a solid barrier without really having the strength to hold a large animal in.

I have been in a round pen built along the lines of that described in the novel, and it could indeed double as a fort. This sort of round pen provides all three barrier types: physical, psychological and visual. You can't see in or out of this sort of round pen, it is stout enough to withstand bodily pressure, and it is tall enough that it can't be jumped, all of which create a psychological barrier.

Most round pens that I've seen are physical and mental but not visual barriers. The round pen that we built for our client is a good example of a stout wooden structure that is tall enough that it creates a psychological barrier, too, but you can still see out of it.

My first round pen was a collection of 10' panels made of heavy rod that was also both a physical and psychological barrier. I chose the panels because friends with draft horses recommended them for strength. Indeed, I've put the panels to use as permanent housing in many cases. However, they are so heavy that I must have help to move them, which is a problem since I often work alone. In our snowy climate here in Colorado, that round pen quickly became unusable because it couldn't be entered and plowed or taken down and plowed easily. I realized I needed one that I could set up and take down by myself to facilitate snow plowing. A client told me that many people he knows have also switched to movable round pens.

After much research, I've ended up with 12' Priefert utility panels and a 4' walk-through gate. The panels, even at 12', are just 58 pounds each, and the gate is 89 pounds. I can set up or take down the entire round pen in less than twenty minutes (unless I'm trudging through deep snow, which makes it take longer). A ride-through gate wasn't important to me, and the panels come apart easily enough that if I need to put something wider than 4' inside the round pen, I separate two panels to create a temporary opening. I first learned of the Priefert brand at a colt starting clinic, when the clinician pushed into the panels and demonstrated that they wouldn't sandwich. I've seen a horse sandwich a round pen made from portable panels, so the demonstration left an impression on me.

The size of my round pen varies, sometimes larger, sometimes smaller, depending on what I am doing and what other uses I've put my panels to. The portable nature of these panels has been very handy. Not only does it facilitate moving the round pen in the winter for snow plowing, but I can also change the location and shape of the round pen to suit my training needs. For instance, I've created a mini-round pen inside a larger paddock so that I could separate ponies at feeding time. And once I had to split a pen in two temporarily to help a geriatric pony get enough to eat.

In the summer I shrink my round pen and use some of the panels to create a water gap in a river for a pasture that otherwise doesn't have water. I can also create a funnel out of the panels to facilitate training foals to load into a trailer. I also use them to create temporary housing around my foaling shed. They aren't intended to be used in permanent housing, and I am always mindful when I leave a stallion in my round pen unattended because the panels just don't create enough of a psychological barrier in my opinion nor are they a stout enough physical barrier for testosterone-charged energy.

I know people who have built arenas rather than round pens. I can easily see where an arena would be appropriate if formal riding is important. Unfortunately, arenas are by nature set in location; I have one friend who rarely uses her arena because it is not conveniently located. I have a small paddock that I can use for riding, so my round pen provides me with the versatility that I need for the types of training that I do.

If I ever go back to having just a single pony that doesn't need much training, maybe then I'd consider living without a round pen. But for now, having a moveable one is an indispensable tool in my partnership with my ponies.

---

1)   Hagy, Alyson. *Boleto, A Novel*. Gray Wolf Press, Minneapolis, Minnesota, 2012, p. 42.

ORGANIZING THE DAY

Early in my pony career, an acquaintance loaned me a book that she had found while visiting England. *The Last Horsemen* was particularly interesting to me because it was about a family that uses draft animal power on their farm, Clydesdale horses in particular. One lesson from the book stood out above all others: each day's work revolved around the horses, even though the cash crops of the farm didn't include the horses at all. My memory is that the cash crops of the farm were turnips and other feed crops, yet each day was structured around using the horses to do the work of the farm. This was a novel idea to me; for most of my adult life up to that time, my days had been structured around a 9-to-5-type job and vacations therefrom. To focus one's day around motive power instead of money-making seemed radical. After a dozen years working ponies in harness, the logic is readily apparent to me, yet putting the concept into practice is still a challenge.

The year 2010 was especially challenging. For the first time since I had begun using my ponies commercially, we did not have a horse-logging job. All of our clients pulled back their expenditures, and since horse-logging is the most expensive of the services we offer, it's hardly surprising that interest in it would decline. The result was that I didn't have pressure from the business to work my ponies, and they weren't worked on the farm either because the business was taking most of my time. Yet working my ponies provides me with so much satisfaction that the lesson from *The Last Horsemen* was increasingly on my mind. How could I organize my days around using the ponies, even though money-making activities took me away from them?

I know I'm not alone in this dilemma because I get emails a couple of times a year from people who want to put their ponies to work. I got an email from a friend who bought one of my ponies, and she too was frustrated by some logistics that were keeping her from putting him to work as she'd planned. While I don't think she's read *The Last Horsemen*, she certainly put its lesson to use. She harnessed her pony and ground-drove him out to pick up trash along the highway. The pony carried the plastic bags of trash and quickly learned the routine of walking, stopping, standing while his owner picked up discarded beer cans and put them in his bags, then went on to the next bit of trash.

An implementation of the lesson from *The Last Horsemen* was to use my ponies for commuting. We were working three-quarters of a mile from home, and there was grazing available at the work end of the commute. In the morning, I loaded my portable electric fence corral on my husband's work truck along with several buckets of water. Then when it was time for me to leave for work, I jumped on a pony and went. While I could have used a single pony for commuting, there was enough grazing for three, so I rode one and ponyed two. While ponying didn't provide as much handling as the ponies could have used, at least it was something. By the second day, the ponies knew the routine and we clopped down the road with purpose, me and my troika. I was quite pleased with myself for organizing my non-pony work-day around using my ponies.

HORSEMAN'S JINGLE

During one particularly wintry winter, I had the good fortune to participate in Jerry Williams' Horseman's Jingle. A combination of on-line and phone, individual and group coaching, it was a great source of inspiration and motivation when the elements made life a little more challenging than usual.

One feature of the Jingle was a weekly 'Can You.' Though Jerry was in Florida, he recognized many of us were in less temperate places, so he gave us exercises that could be done in stalls, barns, and paddocks and with tack that didn't mind snow or rain.

The first one was 'Touch it with the tail.' This involved backing my mare Lily into things, paying careful attention to when she got uncomfortable. She was pretty comfortable with everything since in draft work I'm constantly backing ponies into weird situations. I backed Lily up against a tree branch, then up against the horse trailer, then up against the round pen fence, each time until her tail touched the object.

The second 'Can You' was 'Lift a Foot w/ a Snap.' I laughed a little over this one, as it was advertised as being appropriate for inclement days. Have you ever tried snapping your fingers with gloves on, or taking your gloves off at five degrees to snap your fingers?! Lily was great about lifting her front feet when I snapped my fingers, but we had room for improvement with her back feet.

Another 'Can You' was 'Over a pole one foot at a time.' Many people in the Jingle found this one challenging, as their poles were all buried by snow. I managed to find a loose fence rail that I could temporarily relocate, but my challenge became open ground. We resorted to working on this one on the driveway when it was plowed, which was only occasionally because we had a foot and a half of snow in less than a week. Jerry mentioned that this exercise will expose all kinds of things about our relationships with our horses, and he was right. Eventually Lily and I got this one, including the 'extra credit' of straddling the pole, which Lily found easier than walking over the pole one foot at a time on command, pausing between each step until I asked for her to proceed.

Spending time with my ponies always makes me a better companion for the humans in my life. So the best part about these Can You's was making me get out there with them even when the weather was contrary.

THE IRONY OF SKIDDING IN TELLER CITY

In April of 2005, a microburst of wind hit the ghost town of Teller City in the Routt National Forest of Colorado. Thousands of trees were blown down, many of which started their life as Teller City's heyday was drawing to a close around 1885. Now a designated historic site, after the blowdown Teller City became the focus of a salvage timber sale. A special horselogging unit was designated around the highest density of archaeological remains.

According to *The Medicine Bow Mining Camps* by Mel Duncan, between 1880 and 1885 Teller City was large enough to warrant a post office to service an anticipated gold and silver mining boom. (1) Population estimates ranged from 300 to 1200 people at its peak, making Teller City the largest town in the county at the

time. The remains of log cabins are still visible, as are foundations that underlaid framed structures. Streets that once funneled traffic amongst the buildings are still evident. Only a single chimney is in evidence, suggesting that most buildings were heated with wood stoves. An interpretive sign at the site states that there were two newspapers and over twenty saloons present. Teller City seems to have had a very quick rise and fall. One story in Duncan's book tells of the Yates Hotel having no available rooms when I.S. Bartlett arrived, so the proprietor had a room constructed while the guest waited: "The windows and door were put in and the boarding of the walls completed while we occupied the room." A precipitous drop in the price of silver in 1884 caused Teller City to be nearly abandoned overnight, with dirty dishes left on tables and clothes left in closets. (2)

We became acquainted with the blowdown in Teller City in 2005 when we were contacted by US Forest Service timber sale planner Carl Maass. Carl was in search of information about horselogging as a way to protect the cultural resources at the site. We visited Teller City a few times, and our logging company purchased the timber sale in 2006.

In hindsight, this sale was very much about making lemonade out of lemons. When we bought it, I had great hopes about showing how the methods of yesterday could be used to do the work of today. Because of the size of the timber, I considered buying a big team of horses or hiring a teamster and team to help us. The US Forest Service wanted to bring in film crews, and we looked forward to an enjoyable job in a special place. Unfortunately the log market fell apart when a mountain pine beetle epidemic settled in, and the economic downturn didn't help. So we got creative with winches from our mechanical equipment and skidding 16' logs with my ponies.

One glass of lemonade came one September when the US Forest Service invited us to help with a special event. They hosted the kindergarten and first grade classes from our local elementary school for a field trip to Teller City. Our horselogging was a stop on the tour. When I heard the ages of the kids in advance, I decided to bring my littlest pony who is very kid-friendly. After skidding a pole from the woods to the kids with Mya, I let the kids who weren't allergic or afraid feed Mya a small treat. By the last group of visitors, Mya knew

exactly where to stop! We also gave out stickers showing Mya skidding past an old cabin, which we were told were a hit. It was a very fun morning, and it was made even more special when we got a lovely note from the first grade teacher telling us all her students now wanted to be loggers. I just hope they take lots of money management classes while they're in school!

Another glass of lemonade came from the place itself. We have worked all over our large county, and some places, frankly, we'd rather not go back to. It hasn't been because of the people or the work but because of the place itself. I've been in other ghost towns in Colorado and haven't been inclined to return, but Teller City is different. It is a very special, enjoyable place to be.

From a teamster's perspective, the project had its challenges. I spent a lot of time doing advance scouting of skid trails because of the variety of hazards we encountered. The density of rusted cans and broken glass was higher than most places we work. And there were of course foundations and fallen-down log cabins to avoid. An interpretive trail with signs built in the 1990s is a wonderful benefit to the visiting public, but we had to take care to clear it of downed trees without damaging it. And then there were the caved-in outhouse holes that hid easily behind tree trunks. Easier to see but still occasionally surprising were open cellars. And one day we came across a grave with a plaque bearing the Psalm of David. The lemonade from all this is knowing that we did a careful job in a special place.

As I drove the long commute to Teller City each day, I pondered an article I had read about the 2007 US Department of Agriculture Census. (3) In reviewing the Census, Chet Kendell found that the most profitable farms were those that provided the sole source of income to their operators. Part-time farmers, hobby farmers, and retirement farmers weren't as successful at turning a profit. There appears to be an important link between being full time and dependent on a place and seeing how to make it successful. After we bought the Teller City Salvage Sale, I became a part-time farmer. I took time off from my animals to help our logging company survive this challenging project. I watched my work ponies grow fat and my farm income decline. It feels ironic somehow that a horselogging project would distract me from horses. The glass of lemonade here is returning to my farm the wiser.

(1) Duncan, Mel. *The Medicine Bow Mining Camps*. Jelm Mountain Publications, Laramie, Wyoming, 1990, p. 89.
(2) Peterson, Mary, Forest Supervisor, Medicine Bow/Routt National Forest. "The Tale of Teller City," http://www.fs.fed.us/r2/mbr/resources/heritage/routt_history_6_teller%20city.pdf, 2005.
(3) Kendell, Chet. "Farming from the Heart: Livelihoods that Hinge on the Land," *Small Farmers Journal*, Summer 2009, Vol. 33, No. 3, p. 35.

QUICK RELEASE STRATEGIES

I had the ponies tied as I usually do prior to feeding vitamin buckets. As I was retrieving the buckets to go back over the fence with them to the ponies, out of the corner of my eye I saw a pony acting strangely. When I looked, she had tangled her head in her lead rope. I set the buckets down and headed her direction quickly, trying to reassure her with words as I approached. This wasn't just a typical tangle; she had somehow wrapped the leadrope twice around the throatlatch part of her neck and then pulled it tight.

I was reminded as I freed her from her predicament the importance of having multiple quick release strategies in situations where ponies tangle themselves when tied. Generally, we're advised as horse owners to never tie our equines long or low, to avoid them tangling themselves in their lead ropes. When I'm feeding them buckets while tied, I have to tie a little longer than normal so that they can reach their buckets on the ground.

Having multiple quick release strategies for when ponies tangle themselves in their lead rope is important in case the first one fails, as was the case this time. The pony had wrapped the lead rope so tight around her neck that I couldn't get to the breakaway snap that is designed to be easy to release even when there is pressure on it. So I resorted to my second quick release strategy: the quick release knot on the lead rope. It, too, is designed to come free even when there's pressure on it, and I've only rarely had it give me trouble. It worked as it was supposed to in this situation, and I was able to free the pony from the tangle she had created.

I always carry a pocket knife, which was another quick release strategy if I needed it, as I could have cut the lead rope if necessary. And there is another strategy that I consider so basic that I forget about it. It is really critical to be extra watchful when tying ponies long. Especially with expressive ponies, either by tossing their heads (as was the case this time) or pawing, they can so easily tangle themselves. With any pony, though, I consider it my ultimate responsibility to keep an eye on them when they are tied long to make sure their creativity doesn't get them in trouble.

PONYING

Because I'm interested in the various types of work that ponies can do – ride, drive, draft, pack – I have found that ponying is helpful in preparing youngsters for any of these jobs, and it can be begun shortly after weaning.

For ponying to be enjoyable, of course, the young pony should be trained to lead willingly, and especially if they have more whoa than go, it helps if they are accustomed to trotting in hand. In addition, the young pony and riding pony should be acquainted with each other, preferably housed together in a paddock where they can sort out personal space issues and relative pecking order so that you don't have to manage those sorts of interactions while riding.

Because I use a lot of voice commands with my ponies, ponying is a great way to introduce those commands to a young pony by using them to instruct the pony you're riding. Then, when the young pony is ready for riding or driving work, they're already familiar with the meaning of walk, trot, whoa, and lope. Even if you don't intend to use voice commands later on, I've found that using voice commands that are familiar when teaching riding and driving helps the young pony to pick up on the purpose of their work more quickly.

My most frequent use of ponying isn't very glamorous. I use it to move multiple ponies from one place to another, typically from pasture to horse trailer or home. Trail rides are my principal experience with recreational ponying. It's a great way to get a young pony out 'in the world' and to spend time with them and have fun with them before they can be formally used. You do, of course, have to manage differing reactions to stimuli, which in my case includes the odd moose, bear, or tree falling, or my dog pouncing on something in the brush. While your riding pony may be used to these things, remember that your young pony may not be. It can of course be helpful that the young pony will pick up on how the older pony reacts, so it makes sense to use your most reliable mount as your riding pony.

A driving instructor once suggested that I 'pony' a pony I had in training with one of my work ponies to get her accustomed to different types of 'vehicles.' She got to experience work carts, stone boats, and jog carts behind her this way without being hitched. Another time I ponied a young pony from a jog cart for an exhibition where people wanted to see a Fell Pony but I didn't have one trained to drive.

One extremely handy use of ponying has been exercising young colts after gelding. My vet recommends at least thirty minutes of exercise at least once a day for a week to ten days after castration to ensure that swelling doesn't develop at the wound site. And it definitely helps. When I first did this, I ponied the colt from its dam. The next time I ponied a colt from his father who was still a stallion at the time. Using ponying for post castration exercise made for a more enjoyable enforced exercise routine for me and the new gelding. I'm not sure the riding pony necessarily agreed!

TRAILERING

Based on the number of articles and DVDs I see, trailer loading is apparently a frequent challenge for horse owners. My first Fell Pony taught me to not take trailer loading for granted, as she refused to load by herself in a two-horse straight-load trailer. When we removed the center divider, she was fine, but when we later tried to load her in the trailer with another horse with the center divider in its normal position, she would have nothing of it.

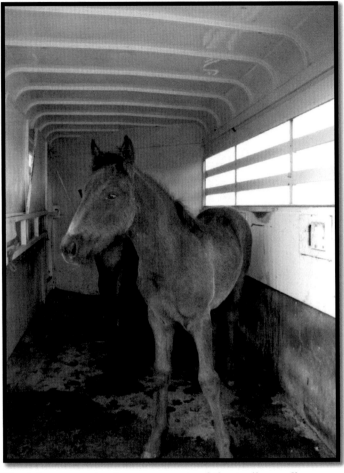

When I had to move her from Turkey Trot Springs to Willowtrail Farm with a foal at foot, we tried again to load she and her foal in a two horse trailer with the divider removed. She threw such a fit a mile into the journey that we had to unload her and walk her back to our starting point. I ultimately had to borrow a three-horse slant load trailer with the dividers stowed to make the six-and-a-half hour trip. Now I have a three-horse-slant of my own, and she will travel with other ponies as long as she gets to stand backwards in a stall. Since her face is exposed to the outside when loaded this way, it only works for short distances. For long distances, I haul her loose and alone or put Plexiglas panes in the open part of the trailer wall.

Fortunately, none of my other ponies have proved as challenging in the trailering department as that first Fell. But since I know not to take trailer loading for granted, and because my farm situation requires that my ponies travel in trailers regularly, trailer loading is a skill that I teach all my ponies, young and old.

A frequently requested article on my website is "Teaching Foals to Trailer Load," which describes the many approaches to the topic that I have used over the years. The number one key to foals learning to trailer load is of course having their dams do so quietly and willingly.

Especially being a breeder, when I ship ponies to all corners of North America, I think it's important that my ponies load willingly and can do it at all times of the day and in all sorts of weather. More than one pony has left here in a snow storm!

From a pony's perspective, I do have to admit that it takes a lot of trust and courage to ride inside a metal box that makes noise, shakes, and travels at great rates of speed. I am very thankful for my ponies that load easily and travel well.

THE MEANING OF HALTERS

Several years ago, one of my mentors was a breeder of Quarter Horses. She had a stallion that was in demand for breeding to outside mares. She and her husband had a special breeding area built in their barn. And they always used a special halter when bringing Mac to the barn so he knew what was expected of him. It was clear that Mac knew the difference between that halter and the everyday variety: his behavior changed markedly. He was normally placid but got excited as expected (and required!) when the special halter was put on.

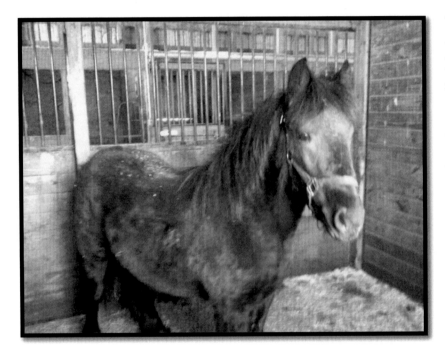

When I brought home a new colt who traveled all the way from Scotland, I learned something else about the meaning of halters. Lucky Joe was just seven months old when he began his journey and arrived here after 55 days on the road. I wondered how long it would take him to know that he was finally home to stay. I figured it would be a week or two; a friend said he thought it would take just two days. It never occurred to me that the act of removing his halter for the first time in 55 days might tell him something, but it clearly did. He instantly looked at me differently.

My friend and colleague Doc Hammill instructs students in Gentle Horsemanship with a special emphasis on driving and draft equines. Doc is adamant about halters being left on horses under their work bridles with lead ropes attached. In the article "Hitching Safely" in *Rural Heritage* magazine, Doc tells about being in the process of hitching a team during a clinic when a bolt of lightning hit nearby, causing one horse to jump and then fall, taking the lines with him. Doc said about this extreme teaching moment, "It's unlikely that I would have been able to hang onto and control both horses if I had not had halters and lead ropes on them. I was able to quickly undo the ropes from the hames and use them instead of the lines (which became useless because the fallen horse was lying on them). Without halters on AND lead ropes attached and easily accessible, we are at an extreme disadvantage if someone needs to get control of the heads." (1)

Doc's advice is echoed by William Castle in *Heavy Horse World* magazine. Castle began his article by telling a tragic story he'd seen in the local paper about a pony being killed when the halter it was wearing while at pasture became entangled and the pony broke its neck trying to free itself. Castle went on to say, "There is another reason not to turn a horse out wearing a halter. When I put a halter on a horse, it is a signal that I am now in charge. If I say 'whoa' I want him to stay where he is, even if I am only loosely holding the lead rope or have dropped it on the ground… After work, taking the halter off is the signal that he can now do as he pleases. If I were to leave the halter on I am undoing the valuable lesson that a halter means he has to do as he is told." (2)

That halters on and off can carry such significant meaning has profound implications for our work with ponies. If we assume the role that Castle suggests, that we are now in charge, then we of course have a responsibility as leader of our herd of two to watch out for our other herd member. In my situation where my ponies are kept in herds, if I have only haltered one pony of several in a paddock, it's my responsibility, for instance, to protect that pony from all the other ponies in the herd who are loose. It is a poor reflection on my leadership if I allow my haltered pony to be pushed on, bit, or kicked or in any way threatened by the ponies that are unrestrained. Undoubtedly Doc's ability to maintain control of his horses in the extreme situation he found himself in was due in part to the horses understanding that they were to listen to him as leader. In fact, one student observed, "The horses stayed relatively calm because they felt that from Doc; they knew they needed to just stop and stand while he made things right." (3)

Castle concluded his article with a bit of humor to punctuate the lesson, "As to whether I always follow my own advice, I did once forget to take a halter to the field, and on that occasion harnessed up without a halter. Even though I did not need it... it felt as uncomfortable as if I had forgotten to wear underpants. Although no-one could tell, it felt very unsafe; and what would I have done in an emergency?" (4)

Putting halters on and taking halters off can mean "I'm breeding" or "I'm home" or "I'm working." When you halter and unhalter your pony, what do you communicate? When your pony has a halter on, do you sense a different relationship with him or her than when they are loose-headed? The longer I am around ponies, the less I take for granted.

---

1)   Morrissey, Jenifer. "Hitching Safely," *Rural Heritage* magazine, December 2012/January 2013, p. 18.
2)   Castle, William. "Halters on, halters off," *Heavy Horse World*, Summer 2013, p. 20
3)   Morrissey, p. 12
4)   Same as #2.

LEADING FROM THE OFF SIDE

I've learned that equines need to be taught things on both sides of their bodies, and I have found that just because a pony leads well with me on their left doesn't necessarily mean that they will lead well when I'm on their right. So I try to make sure that all my ponies get used to me leading them from both the near and off sides.

I was bringing the ponies home from pasture one day, which involves loading them in my three-horse slant-load trailer. The natural angle and approach to loading the trailer is from the near side, but when the wind is blowing towards me, it blows the door towards me, blocking the pony's path and creating a safety hazard. The day that I chose to bring the ponies home was of course windy and added to that, there was snow. The wind was blowing the snow sideways, pelting me and the ponies as well as blowing the door of the trailer shut.

To load the ponies that day, I had to hold the trailer door open, which put me on the off-side of the ponies for loading. Here was the first time I was glad that they were used to being led from the off-side. I sent each pony into the trailer from their off side, then threw the leadrope on their back, and climbed in and around next to them on their near side, retrieving and tying the leadrope as usual.

That day because I was in a hurry because of the weather, I loaded that set of three ponies in a different order than I usually do. They immediately began fidgeting and expressing displeasure about their different placement in the trailer. It was clear I had to undo what I'd done, so I unloaded the fidgety ones and reloaded them in the proper order. When I finally closed the door on the trailer (with the help of the wind), I was DOUBLY glad these ponies load from the offside since two of them had to be loaded twice, in driving snow!

TO TREAT OR NOT TO TREAT

After reading various Parelli Natural Horsemanship publications about using treats as training aids, it appears that the Parellis have been taken to task by people who consider treats as vices not aids. I most appreciated Linda Parelli's comeback: those folks who are throwing stones had best not have a horse to train who is a thinker rather than a doer, has more whoa than go, and needs motivation. Discounting treats as a training aid with this sort of equine is throwing out a potentially valuable motivational tool when dealing with a challenging personality.

I knew exactly the type Linda was describing when I read her comeback because the description perfectly fit my first pony. For the first year that I had her, I tried to get her to bond with me by going out to visit her right before bed and offering her a treat. Sometimes she would come out of her barn to get it and sometimes that was more bother than a little treat was worth. I've since bonded deeply with that pony; I can ride her bareback without a halter or lead rope through a pasture. Treats are my friend on such journeys. And I've  taken to heart the distinction the Parellis make between using treats as bribe and using them as motivation. My use of them at the barn at night definitely qualified as bribe. On journeys across the pasture, I used them as motivation and reward.

Now I have a whole herd of ponies, and there are a few others that qualify for treats during training. Most, however, do not. Any pony that exhibits mouthiness is disqualified, which so far has meant none of my males - stallions, colts or geldings - get treats. Some of my mares also are disqualified for the same reason. I have found a way to use treats with one of my mouthiest ponies after pondering the Parelli point of making their use motivation. When I think the pony needs motivation, I set a treat somewhere on the ground and then point him at it until he finds it. He usually turns to me much more interested in the next task at hand.

The treats I use are actually not marketed as treats. They're a complete-feed-wafer intended to be a regular feed for horses so they're low in sugar and low in protein, though higher in both than the hay that is my ponies' predominant feed. I got a good laugh one day regarding treats: I keep a container of treats in the tack room of my trailer. It is a six-inch wide plastic tub with a screw top. One day at work, one of my work ponies that definitely isn't supposed to get treats stuck his head in the tack room when I wasn't paying attention and figured out how to unscrew the container of treats. He was in heaven. When I worked him a half hour later, I had a challenge on my hands because he was high on concentrated feed!

One of the Parelli perspectives on using treats has given me pause. They say that treats are a tool to use until your horsemanship improves to a point where you no longer need to use them. I wonder if my first pony will live long enough for me to improve that much!

The picture shows Lily earning a treat as reward. I taught her to 'shake' on voice command in less than 24 hours because she was so motivated to get a treat.

PATTERN WATCHERS

Several years ago I was watching a team lay flagstone as a foundation for a wall. Each piece of rock was shaped uniquely, and the team was putting great effort into making the rocks fit snugly together. One of the people at work was a professional pattern maker; her craft was to create patterns for outdoor clothing for companies like Patagonia and Columbia. I grew up sewing clothes, so I was familiar with what clothes patterns were. I had also made enough of my own clothes to know that translating a picture of a garment onto a square of fabric and transforming it into something wearable seemed almost magical to me. This woman's ability to see shapes and opportunities for placement while laying the flagstone far exceeded anyone else's on the job.

While this person's ability to recognize and use patterns seemed extraordinary to me at the time, I've since learned that my ponies far exceed most humans in their ability to recognize patterns. My Fell Ponies seem to be especially adept in this department. My first two Fells, Beauty and Midnight, were the ones who taught me that they recognized patterns. Shortly after I got them, I put them in a new pasture. I acquainted them with the perimeter fence, as well as where to find water, but about an hour later they were standing at the gate looking at me. It slowly dawned on me that they were thirsty. While I had put water out for them and showed them where it was, their intent looks over the gate made it clear that something was amiss. I then realized that they had identified a pattern and I hadn't followed it. In every other enclosure that I had ever put them in, I put the water at the gate. In this enclosure, I put it in a different place. Despite showing the water to them, they had used their knowledge of my past pattern of water provision, and the water wasn't where they expected; it wasn't at the gate.

Another Fell Pony, Ellie, showed me her own understanding of patterns. Before Ellie got her morning bucket of vitamins, I tied her to the fence in a particular place. When she saw me approaching with buckets, she came to the fence to greet me. I then climbed through the fence with her halter. Instead of letting me halter her there, though, she moved off to the section of fence where she knew she was to be tied, waiting for me to come and complete the task.

These examples, of course, illustrate that the ponies watch my patterns. Beauty and Midnight, in fact, communicated to me what my pattern was; until that morning when they were thirsty I didn't realize that I had a pattern of always putting water at the gate!

As I've spent more time with my ponies, I've realized that the fact that they are pattern watchers is an important tool in training. I can show them a certain sequence of things repeatedly and they become accepting of it. A few years ago, Parelli Natural Horsemanship published an entire training methodology utilizing patterns.

I used patterns to solve a small problem with Ellie. One morning when I approached the fence with vitamin buckets, she greeted me but then walked off and didn't let me halter her. It was unusual as she was usually willing to be haltered at any time. I realized that the pattern I had established during this morning routine was to tie her but then wait to give her a bucket after the rest of the ponies in the paddock had received theirs. I changed my pattern to give her a bucket first, before the rest of the herd. From then on, I had no problem haltering her.

On my pony journey, I've learned that not all ponies are alike. My first Fells were mellow but not as confident as my first two ponies. My first two non-Fell Ponies were so confident that I extrapolated from them to my Fells after I got them. When I used the same training techniques on my Fells that I'd used previously, they didn't work as well.

The patterns that Parelli Natural Horsemanship has developed are intended to help with developing confidence. After studying them for a time and not seeing anything particularly special, I realized that it is patterns in general that are important in developing confidence. Patterns are important because ponies are pattern watchers.

One month I was working with my pony Matty on a daily basis. Everyday I did the same thing again that I had done the day before, perhaps with one small variation. I established patterns, and Matty showed that she appreciated the approach. She

recognized and took comfort from the consistency, and we slowly but steadily made progress. She showed me that just because she's mellow doesn't mean that she's bold and fearless like my first two ponies. She needs to be convinced that what we're doing is safe, and using patterns helps her develop that confidence.

Understanding that ponies are pattern watchers has taught me a lot about myself. If they respond to me in an unexpected way, I then ponder whether I've shown them some pattern that they're reflecting back to me. If I can find the pattern, or on the other hand if I've deviated from a pattern I've established, and I can change myself, I can improve our relationship.

I've come to realize that I'm a pattern watcher myself and that's one reason why I find the ponies so fascinating. And it's not just the ponies. My ducks are pattern-watchers, too. They know the difference between me coming out of the house with carrot tops in my hand and coming out with a tray of lettuce leaves. They know the lettuce leaves are headed for them, and they start voicing their approval! Both the ponies and the ducks can teach me by doing something unusual or they can show me something I wouldn't have seen otherwise. Life with animals is so interesting, and much more so now that I understand patterns.

TAILS TO THE GATE

What does it mean when four ponies are standing with tails to the gate and ears pricked at attention despite the fact that I'm approaching with feed buckets and I've just put out fresh hay? Normally either hay or buckets are sufficient to draw at least one pony's attention to me.

I faced this mystery on the first sunny calm morning after a couple of weeks of clouds, blowing snow, and wind. Fortunately there were four pairs of clues: those adorable pony ears were pointing to the source of the problem. A yearling moose was eating their hay.

I continued to the adjoining paddock to complete the chores there, all the while contemplating how to deal with the problem. I considered chasing the moose off myself, but that was only a temporary solution. I've learned that the moose know my patterns, and they return when they know I'm not around. I settled on bringing Torrin up to the problem paddock, as I know he won't tolerate competition for hay.

Meanwhile, in the problem paddock, I was aware of four sets of pony feet occasionally and quickly changing position, with accompanying snorts and plumes of steam. I stopped to watch the situation before I embarked on implementing my chosen solution, and I was thrilled to see another solution present itself. My younger Norwegian Fjord gelding Randver began approaching the moose. He was tentative at first but got bolder and more resolute as he saw the moose back off. I cheered Randver on, and within minutes all four ponies were peacefully eating their hay. I haven't seen the moose in that paddock since.

I never have a camera when such a drama is unfolding, of course. Instead I've included a picture of a younger Randver watching a cow moose (look behind the shed.)

HORSE RESEARCH IN ACTION

One morning I read an article about some horse-related research, and shortly thereafter I got to see it in action. It was midday, and a snow storm was blowing in when I went out to feed. The seven ponies in the turnout were in high spirits with the change in weather, and the youngest were charging around, rearing, and tussling with each other.

The article I read was titled "Young Horses Behave Better Around Adults," and indeed I was appreciative of my older mares. They exert a calming influence on the rambunctious youngsters, so entering the turnout isn't quite as exciting as it would be otherwise on a day like that day. "…adult horses play a pivotal role in channeling the aggressive behavior of immature herd mates…. Anti-social activities were four times more common in groups where juveniles outnumbered adults, compared with those herds with the highest proportion of adults." (1)

It's not that the older mares don't get into the fun, but they tend to come down from the high faster than the younger ones. There have been a few times when I've had a large proportion of young ponies together, and it doesn't take me long to figure out that I wanted to add older ponies to the mix. Herdmates are together a lot more of the day than I am with them, so if I can mix my herd up from an age perspective, more socialization training gets done than I can ever do by myself. I try to keep at least one mare with my stallions for the same reason.

Some mares are better than others at discipline, and it seems to be related to position in the herd. The more dominant mares are more likely to 'tell off' youngsters than those lower in the 'pecking order.' I was surprised when I put together a video entitled 'Mothers & Daughters.' The pictures I had of my mare Val were noticeably different than those of my other mares. Val was a great mother, but she was a bit permissive for my tastes. The pictures in the video all show her distant from her daughter, and the pictures of the other mare-and-daughter pairs show the mares much closer to their daughters. When she was here, Val was always the bottom mare, and her offspring required more of my attention in socialization.

I enjoyed watching the ponies cavort that day in the snowstorm, both young and old. And when I entered their midst with a tub of hay, I didn't have as much concern for my safety thanks to my mares. They were ready to get down to the business of eating without much delay, and the youngsters followed suit with only a few extra bucks and kicks.

---

1.   http://www.horsesciencenews.com/horse-behavior/young-horses-behave-better-around-adults.php

MINDING THE LEADERS

One morning Ellie didn't come to me to be haltered as she normally does. I don't know why; perhaps it was the wind in the air or the fresh dusting of snow or extra hunger from a colder morning or lots of mud. Instead of coming to greet me at the fence when I appeared, she went off and stood where I normally tie her while she gets her vitamin bucket. I could have just walked over to her and haltered and tied her since she was where I would put her anyway, but I didn't. Ellie's change in behavior felt like a test of me as a leader. I accepted the gauntlet. Instead of walking up to her and haltering her, I waited until she came to me. It took some effort on my part, but in the end I know it had benefits.

I had recently read some research about which horses in a herd other horses mimic. "Horses can learn how to do something simply by observing another horse. But they'll only readily pick up the new behavior if they have a certain relationship with the horse they're watching." Not surprisingly, the research found that dominant horses are more likely to be copied, as are horses that are familiar. Submissive horses and unknown horses were less likely to induce mimicking behavior. (1)

Whenever I'm with my ponies, I'm on the lookout for changes in behavior. Ellie is the leader of the herd in her paddock, and her change in behavior was not only about our relationship but also about my relationship with every other pony in the herd. How I dealt with her insubordination would have ramifications with the rest of the ponies that were watching, as the research indicated. It was actually somewhat comical because three of the youngstock came up to me wanting to stick their heads in the halter the way that Ellie normally does. Perhaps they were mimicking her normal behavior, not the behavior she was exhibiting that morning.

In addition to benefiting my relationship with the rest of the herd, my persistence in making Ellie come to me paid off in my relationship with her. The next morning I sat on her back for the first time. She showed absolutely no indication that my presence there was an issue. It was a major thrill.

(1)   "Horses selective in who they copy," http://www.horsesciencenews.com/horse-behavior/horses-selective-in-who-they-copy.php

HORSES AND HALTERS IN PHOTOGRAPHS

One morning I looked at an equine calendar, and the March illustration made me smile. It was a photograph of a mare and foal running in a pasture, and the mare was wearing a halter. It made me smile because seeing horses in halters but no lead ropes in photographs brings to mind lots of questions.

For instance, in the photograph I saw, was the halter left on the mare to show how domesticated she is? Or was it left on because the owner couldn't catch her to take it off and the photo was snapped as she and the foal ran about free? I have heard of ponies who have worn halters for months because their owners either couldn't get them off or were afraid if they took them off, they'd never get them back on again. (My first pony taught me that I could walk around a pasture for a long time playing the haltering game if she wanted me to. I learned to play the game differently and can halter her anytime I want now.)

When I see photos of foals wearing halters with no lead rope attached, I have lots of questions, too. Is the owner communicating that the foal is halter broke? Or have they been unable to get the halter off the foal after they got it on the first time? I've chased a few foals in my time to know the possibilities! (I've learned that the best solution is to stay still and wait, as inevitably the foal's curiosity will take over, and it will come to me and let me take the halter off.) Unfortunately I've heard stories of foals being injured by halters being left on. These stories make my questions feel more serious.

Unless my ponies are being handled or worked, I rarely leave halters on them and therefore rarely take photos of them with halters on. Do people wonder if my ponies are halter-broke? It's a reasonable question, I suppose. The reality is that they are so halter-broke that when I appear with a halter and lead rope, they try to stick their nose through even if they're not the pony I was intending to halter.

One day my husband came home at lunch to find me in the turnout with seven ponies tied to the fence. He said it was a pretty amusing scene. He ought to have been there when I first entered the turnout with seven halters over my arm! I immediately had five ponies approach me wanting to have their halter put on first. I was pretty impressed that among the five was the youngest. The two mares that didn't approach on this occasion concluded that I wasn't worth that much attention. On the other hand, another mature mare was the first to approach me. It's clear for which mares I need to improve my horsemanship!

I doubt that I will change my haltering habits or my photographing habits when it comes to ponies and halters. Hopefully people will ask me about whether my ponies are halter-broke when they see pictures of them running free not wearing halters. And if other people choose to share photographs of their equines wearing halters, I'll continue to ponder the questions the photos bring to mind.. Questions are great additions to my life.

MANAGING HERD DYNAMICS FOR SAFETY

While hay feeding provides me with lots of behavior to watch, feeding vitamin buckets in the morning is even more fascinating. Eager jostling for a bucket creates a serious safety issue both for the ponies and for me because someone is likely to get kicked. I can usually manage four, and five is possible only if they all get along. All my ponies are taught to back up to receive their buckets, which generally protects me, but there is still jostling for position that puts the ponies, especially the smaller ones, at risk. With seven ponies in a

paddock, the solution has been to tie the five oldest ponies to the fence prior to bringing in the buckets.

Safety is still of paramount importance, so I always tie the most dominant pony first, assuring that she can't bully the others when they are constrained. I then work my way down the herd hierarchy for the same reason. After several weeks, the ponies normally present themselves in proper order to be haltered and tied. The order of release is equally important for safety, so the least dominant is untied first. I'm always touched when one of the ponies chooses to stay with me for a few private minutes of scratching before heading off to their morning hay.

The ponies get to know the routine well enough that they are waiting at the fence when I approach with the halters. If Beauty isn't at the bottom of the stairs where I go through the fence, I know she will be along shortly, pushing the other ponies away. To protect myself from getting trampled by a herd of moving ponies as

I go through the fence, I always wait for Beauty to clear the rail. The picture shows Beauty after she's cleared the rail and is awaiting my approach.

I know I am very fortunate to live with my ponies. Many people have to board their equines and don't get to watch them continuously. Since I never know what life will hand out, I try to give thanks every day for the gift of being with my ponies. It is gift that I treasure.

MAMA SEE, MAMA DO

I have heard many discussions over the years about how much influence mares have on their foals in terms of behavior and temperament. Matty and her daughter Libby gave me an opportunity to see this influence in very real terms.

Apparently the pattern was already set when Libby was just a few hours old. This was before they'd even gotten the nursing thing figured out (Libby was Matty's first foal, and Matty has since proven to be a fabulous mother.) I snapped this picture of Libby four hours into life, imitating her mother's position almost exactly.

A few weeks later we were all into a routine that included traveling by trailer to pasture in the morning and returning home to the foaling shed for the night. While the girls were gone at pasture each day, I would clean out the manure and refresh the straw in the shed. When the girls came in at night, the first thing they did when they got off the trailer and into the fresh straw was to squat and urinate in exact unison. It was truly amazing to watch. Unfortunately I was never prepared with the camera.

When Libby was about three weeks old, I introduced her to Rose, a three-year-old filly. Matty was understandably protective, and Rose was curious, but before long they understood how to peacefully share the paddock. On the second day I went out to throw them some hay. Matty pushed Rose off a pile of hay by taking a quick step toward her with her head lowered, her neck outstretched and ears laid back. Rose quickly moved off to the next closest pile. I then watched little Libby do exactly as her mother had done: take a quick step towards Rose with her head lowered and neck outstretched. I thought that was pretty bold of a youngster, but Rose moved off again. I laughed hard then. Libby had once again imitated her mother precisely and in this case had been rewarded for it: Rose acceded to Libby's 'dominance.' (That dominance was definitely context-specific; Rose only acceded because she knew Matty would protect Libby if necessary.)

I took advantage of 'mama see, mama do' when Libby was about two and a half months old. I was trimming Matty's hooves, and Libby was 'helping.' She took things out of my farrier bucket and put them on the ground; she nibbled my jacket; and she tried to play with the electric grinder. At one point I was trimming Matty's hinds when I felt Matty's body shudder behind me. I looked around, and Libby had begun nursing; the shudder I felt was her butting Matty's udder to get milk to flow. Since Libby was obviously watching what I was doing with her mother, I took a break at one point and gave Libby similar attention. I picked up each of her feet and patted them with my hand, which I hadn't done for several weeks. Libby stood compliantly still, once again doing as she saw her mother do.

Certainly there are things that Libby did that her mother hadn't taught her. Libby and her mother were at pasture with four other ponies for several weeks. When I arrived at pasture, Libby was usually the first one to greet me, either leading the herd towards me or making her way around the bigger ponies to get a scratch in her favorite place. Matty rarely asks for attention that overtly, so I recognized this behavior as Libby's own. Libby showed me, though, that I can always learn something new from my ponies, in this case learning that foals have the capacity to imitate their mamas.

SHARING DECISION-MAKING WITH PONIES

I was once asked if my ponies ever like to please or work with me. I responded, "I have several who are definitely in the 'want to please' category, but of course being ponies, their definition of 'please' includes participation in the decision-making process!" I was then asked what that looks like, and I was stopped in my tracks because I'd never had to answer that question succinctly before.

Ask, Not Tell

Fortunately Judith Bean regularly includes this topic when instructing students in horsemanship. "When I

need my pony to make a certain movement, I ask her," says Judith. "I never tell or demand. I am her partner, not her boss! If I get the correct response, then yea, the pony and I are in agreement. If I don't, then I know my pony has misunderstood my request. This is MY fault. I ask again, more clearly or maybe using 'different language', while encouraging my pony's efforts to agree that not only the movement is possible, but a good idea." (1)

Communication

At the root of how Judith works with her pony is the idea that there is two-way communication, not one-way as in 'tell' or 'demand'. Equines are quite accustomed to two-way communication. In fact, Carolyn Resnick found when observing wild horse herds that equines are in a state of continuous communication with their herd-mates:

I became aware that communication between the horses was not an occasional or sporadic occurrence…. [While] I saw the horses as orderly and harmonious, beneath the surface I soon discovered constant dynamics of communication between horses. Ear flicks and tail swishes were part of a communication system. One horse even slightly shifting position conveyed an important message to nearby horses. I learned that harmony among horses is maintained by a constant undercurrent of communication and herd interaction. I eventually saw that for the herd to be in the most harmonious state, communication between the horses must be at its peak. (2)

Judith's ask-and-answer approach acknowledges that ponies naturally communicate with each other. Just as in a herd where there is a back and forth between herd members, there is a back and forth between human and pony, too, whether we know it or not. Our ponies respond to us best when we recognize this interaction and use it instead of the one-way communication of 'tell' or 'demand.'

A Conversation

To practice equestrian art is
to establish a conversation
on a higher level with the horse;
a dialogue of courtesy and finesse.
--Nuno Olivera

The way I think about Judith's ask-and-answer approach is that any time we're with our ponies, we're having a conversation. It may not be in words like we would share with other humans, but it is a conversation nonetheless. I do use words with my ponies, and I know they understand some of them, but they certainly understand more of my body language, my direct contact, and even on occasion my thoughts and intentions.

How Ponies Respond

Sharing decision-making with my ponies means I acknowledge that we are having a conversation whenever I ask for something. It's up to me, of course, to 'listen' for their response. I have found that they respond in one of three ways:

- With a try
- With a question
- With three questions

A try is an attempt to do what we want. These types of ponies I would classify as the 'want to please' variety. A try is of course the easiest for us to respond to because it is an indication of willing compliance. A try allows the next ask to be shaped so that the next try is an even better answer. Progress can be quickly made on our (human) agenda.

A response in the form of a question is feedback to us that our ask wasn't understood, as Judith alluded to. We become better horsemen and horsewomen by learning to answer questions from our ponies, hoping that our next ask is understood and elicits a try. Sometimes there is genuine confusion, as Judith suggested, and sometimes a pony is unconfident and needs to be given reassurance. Being asked questions by my ponies and then answering them is, for me, what sharing decision-making with my ponies looks like.

A response in the form of three questions is what gives ponies, in my opinion, their reputation for being stubborn. In this case, we are being given feedback that we're not being provocative enough with our ask. It's not so much that the pony hasn't understood as that they want to be convinced that any effort put out on their part will be worthwhile. And from the perspective of these types of ponies, the effort goes beyond just physically moving to include ceding authority to us, which I'm convinced is the challenging part for three-questions types.

Any individual pony may respond in any of these ways depending on the circumstances. Generally, though, I've found that individual ponies tend to respond in one of these ways most of the time. For instance, my stallion Robin was definitely in the 'try' category when I worked with him. I rarely saw him in either of the other two categories, making him great fun to train because progress could be made so quickly.

The Ask Returned

My inquirer asked if I have 'ponies wanting to please or work with me.' The day after I got the question, I had a yearling load himself into the horse trailer before I'd even haltered him. I was obviously very appreciative of him doing what I wanted before I'd even asked. This particular pony is a son of Robin and takes after his father by being in the 'try' category.

And then I have ponies that are in the questioning categories. Two mares showed a willingness to please, prefaced by some questions, indicating their desire to have a conversation. In the first case, the mare met me at the fence asking for a treat. Rather than give her one immediately, I recognized an opportunity to further our work together, so I started a conversation about me riding her across the paddock without a halter or lead rope. She responded by asking clarifying questions about what I wanted, resulting in her carrying me to my requested destination on her back.

The second mare was at pasture when I haltered her and mounted her and asked her to carry me to the trailer to go home. She did a well-scripted three-questions routine, asking if she couldn't please go the opposite direction towards the stallion instead. I remained persistent, asking for what I wanted, and after three tries to go the opposite direction, we ended up at the horse trailer. The next time I mounted this mare in the same situation, we went to the horse trailer without questions!

While many ponies will on occasion be three-questions types, there can be bloodlines that are full of the three-questions type of ponies. These ponies are the ones that came to mind when I answered that my ponies like to share in decision-making. These ponies have brought me lots of laughter (when I don't let myself get frustrated) because they often respond to 'asks' in unexpected and creative ways. These types of ponies are a joy to play with, but for performance goals they require a very astute human partner.

Not Just Ponies

It is the very difficult horses that have the most to give you.
--Lendon Gray

It isn't just ponies, of course, that want to share in decision-making by having a prolonged conversation about goals. Linda Parelli talks about her warmblood gelding Allure as one of these types. "[The] key … is not having a rigid focus, but rather maintaining a focus that is flexible and can adjust to what is needed in the moment. Keeping my end goal in mind but allowing Allure to shape how we get there. This often looks like taking his idea and using it to move towards the 'goal'. For example, let's say my goal is to have him stand still and he offers to walk forwards. In this moment there are 2 obvious choices: 1) ask him to stand again, moving him back to the original spot; or 2) move him forwards more, maybe even changing directions, and then give him the opportunity to stand again… Option 2 is where I found harmony with Allure. By encouraging his idea and shaping it towards my goal, we both have smiles on our faces and we both 'win!'"(3)

For a goal-oriented person like me, three-questions types can be challenging until my goal becomes their goal. I found the following quote from Charlotte Angin to be a helpful one since three-questions types are a part of my life: "Each horse that comes into our lives is a gift. There are no accidents in our choosing…, we choose each other for reasons we are often not aware of at the time. Welcome to the journey." (4)

[The] majority of [draft] horses being relied upon [for work] are most likely those of common intelligence, athletic ability and self-motivation. The truly exceptional animals pose too much of a challenge to most of us to presume training... we view them as behavioral problems rather than examples of great intelligence."

– Lynn Miller (5)

Different languages

Judith indicated that if the pony doesn't understand our ask, then it's sometimes necessary to use a "different language" to help the pony understand. Just as there are hundreds of different spoken languages, there are myriad forms of communication with an equine. One of the most commonly used is direct contact – grooming, bits, and legs on sides, for example. Even direct contact, though, has many dimensions. In general, though, contact is a process of applying and then releasing pressure. And the release is the most important part, as Sarah Warne articulates here:

There is a huge difference between a firm and effective rider and a firm and forceful rider. The difference lies in the art of letting go: knowing when to release the pressure, soften the reins, relax the legs. The art of knowing when to say "thank you" and these thank yous must be obvious…. [Even] the best trainer in the world can't tell you exactly when to soften. They can tell you when you should have softened, but as riders we must learn to feel the split second the horse relaxes through his body and accepts what the rider is asking.' (6)

It is that process of learning when to soften, to release pressure, that makes horsemanship a journey rather than a destination. Every pony is different, and with each of them we have an opportunity to learn new ways of communicating via contact.

Releasing Pressure

"You cannot train a horse by shouts and expect it to obey a whisper."
-- Dagobert D. Runes

One easy way to experience a range of contact and how little it really takes to communicate with a pony is the exercise "Move the Snap."(My thanks to Jerry Williams of The Horseman's Jingle for introducing me to this exercise.)   You will need a halter and a lead rope with a heavy snap. The question to be answered is: just how much movement in the snap via the leadrope is necessary before we notice the pony responding, and ultimately how much is necessary to effect movement of the pony's feet?

Moving the snap is an increase in pressure; letting it go so it drops back to vertical is a release. If a pony responds to the movement of the snap with a slight shift in weight, and you release the pressure, you've rewarded the slightest try. Lynn Miller, in *Training Workhorses, Training Teamsters*, says "I look for, and applaud, the smallest evidence of success." (7)

Learning to release pressure is an ongoing process. There can be times when we think we've released the pressure but in fact we've only lessened it. Laura Masterson of 47th Avenue Farm works a team of Belgian horses and shared this example about her very sensitive horse Patty. "Just letting the snap return to vertical isn't enough of a reward for Patty. She needs me to avert my eyes and sometimes turn my shoulders before she'll relax and lick and chew. It's all in the release, and it works best if you really, really mean it." (8)

Lick and Chew

When the horse's jaws are in motion, his mind is at rest.
--Pete Rose

Laura mentioned 'lick and chew' when talking about rewarding her horse Patty. Lick and chew is one way that ponies communicate with us. Lick and chew means they're processing what they've just experienced; if they've just experienced something new and they aren't licking and chewing, they may not have thoroughly understood what was asked of them or they may not know whether their response was appropriate. Lick and chew is a huge reward for us as our pony's partner because it is an indication of understanding.

I have found that three-questions types of ponies are very stingy with their licks and chews. We really have to earn them. And when we do, the chewing may go on for a very long time. Wait it out; it will be shorter next time. I have found myself, while waiting, wondering why it takes so long for the pony to process what we have just done. I suspect the answer has something to do with coming to peace with ceding authority.

I recently had a conversation with a pony that involved both lick and chew and words. I was at pasture at the end of a very hot day. I had just moved my two-month-old foal Honey and her dam to this pasture the night before, and I was especially concerned about how they were doing with the change, especially given the extreme heat. From a distance Honey didn't look quite right to me, but it was dusk, so I walked to her to check more closely. I was relieved to see that her eyes looked good and her nostrils weren't running. I told her I was worried about her and asked if she was okay (using words.) She immediately began licking and chewing, which made me laugh, both in relief and in joy that she had understood and communicated back to me so effectively!

Timing

If the response you get from a horse is not to your liking, most likely the timing is off rather than the aid needing to be stronger…. We know that the timing of aids needs to be given in the moment that a horse is ready to respond. From this approach training takes a backseat to learning how to ask in the right way.

-- Carolyn Resnick (9)

Carolyn Resnick has yet another take on the ask-respond/conversation/shared decision making spectrum: timing is everything. And I have found that timing itself has many dimensions. Are we asking at an appropriate moment? At an appropriate place in the lesson? At an appropriate place in our relationship? For instance, if I am conversing with one pony in a herd and I ask for the pony to back up just as another pony is walking behind them, then my timing is off in the moment, and I need to ask again when the way is clear. An example of timing within the context of a lesson comes from when I was training my first stallion. I found that it always worked better if I did lots of quick changes of direction in our ground work before asking for something new; Midnight wasn't ready to respond until his feet and mind had been engaged through movement. Then there is asking for something that my relationship with my pony isn't yet strong enough to handle. A vivid example that comes to mind is ground driving for the first time. If I haven't properly prepared my pony for working them from behind, it quickly becomes obvious that my timing within the context of our relationship is off for this activity; they will be totally confused and try to turn and face me, for instance, instead of moving away at a walk.

These are just a few of the many ways that we can communicate with our ponies and they with us. Our ponies are looking for communication all the time, so we have unending opportunities to engage them in conversation. Three-questions types, especially, I have found, seem to be always ready for conversation.

Carrot, Stick, and Otherwise

We've all heard the term "fight or flight." Equines are prey animals that prefer to flee if threatened. If cornered, trapped, or otherwise unable to flee, they may resort to struggling or fighting. It's also likely that we've heard the terms 'carrot' and 'stick' used to describe various approaches to training. I think of the 'carrot' approach as manipulating the flight impulse by using incentives to stay instead of flee, and I think of the 'stick' approach as dealing with the fight impulse.

I've never felt that 'fight or flight' gave a comprehensive view of the world, though; what about resting, eating, and procreating? Some studies suggest that horses in a natural setting, for instance, spend sixteen hours or more each day grazing and otherwise nurturing life. How might we interact with equines in ways that are consistent with nurturing life rather than using the limited approaches of carrot and stick? The answer to this question is conversation, the part of the spectrum between no communication at all (flight response) and one-way communication (the fight response).

Why Share Decision–Making?

...earning a willing compliance, rather than extricating submission, results in a far superior work mate. And the only thing required of us to accomplish this is the right attitude – an attitude born of a never-ending quest for understanding.
– Lynn Miller (10)

Understanding our horses doesn't mean we become 'permissive' or that we don't use firmness and discipline when required. It means rather that we open the door to cooperation rather than confrontation, an attitude that leads to successful performance so much more quickly, easily and joyfully than does domination through fear or submission. Such a humane viewpoint often has the unexpected side effect of enriching our whole lives.
– Linda Tellington-Jones (11)

My inquirer asked what sharing decision-making looks like. The simple answer is that it is a conversation between me and my pony using language that we both understand and that is grounded not in bribery or force but in mutual respect. My inquirer asked about ponies wanting to please. In the end, ponies wanting to please happens more often when I share decision-making with them by engaging them in conversation. I am continually seeking to understand how to have better conversations, as Lynn Miller suggests is necessary. And my life is definitely enriched in many, many ways, as Linda Tellington-Jones suggests, by sharing decision-making with my ponies.

1) Bean-Calhoun, Judith. "Decision making," email to Jenifer Morrissey, 7/16/13.

2) Resnick, Carolyn. *Naked Liberty: Memoirs of My Childhood.* Los Olivos, California: Amigo Publications, Inc., p. 2005, p. 149.

3) http://central.parellinaturalhorsetraining.com/2013/05/a-lesson-with-linda-allure/

4) Angin, Charlotte. Equispiritus Facebook page and http://www.thebreathofthehorse.com/

5) Miller, Lynn. *Training Workhorses, Training Teamsters.* Small Farmer's Journal, Inc., Sisters Oregon, 1994, p. 32.

6) http://www.eurodressage.com/equestrian/2012/09/23/classical-training-art-letting-go

7) Miller, p. 95.

8) Morrissey, Jenifer. "Ideas for the Off Season," *Rural Heritage,* February/March 2013, p. 60.

9) Resnick, Carolyn. http://www.carolynresnickblog.com/the-exciting-journey-of-growing-your-ability-in-training horses/

10) Miller, p. 33.

11) Tellington-Jones, Linda. *Getting in TTouch: Understand and Influence Your Horse's Personality.* Trafalgar Square Publishing, North Pomfret, Vermont, 1995, p. 10

REASSURANCE THROUGH TOUCH

I was riding my mare Lily one day when suddenly her head came up, her ears went forward, and she started weaving her head side to side and suggesting she might want to turn and run. I spoke to her reassuringly and stroked her neck while keeping her pointed forward, and eventually she calmed enough that I could dismount safely. I led her towards the object of her concern, and she quickly determined it wasn't worth being concerned about.

This experience brought to mind a discussion about the senses of the horse. The general theme was that eyesight is their least accurate sense, and Lily's head-weaving was an example of her trying to get a fix on what she was seeing. She wasn't able to get satisfaction until after I dismounted and we approached slowly. Where I used to live, there was a particular boulder along the road on the way to the mailbox that had two circular patterns in it. Two different ponies that I rode repeatedly past that boulder were convinced that rock was a monster. I can't really blame them since it did seem to have eyes, but no matter how often we stopped and I kicked that boulder to indicate it wasn't a concern, these ponies gave anxious sideways glances whenever we passed.

The discussion I read about the senses of the horse got me thinking about how we as people communicate with our equines. In particular, how do we communicate reassurance? It had never occurred to me to use their sense of touch to communicate reassurance. I regularly give affection via their sense of touch by scratching ponies in itchy places. But that wasn't even obvious to me for a number of years. My first three ponies weren't interested in hugs or scratches at all. Now after a dozen years I still don't know if or where two of them like to be scratched. Lily falls in this category, too.

144

I learned that foals like to be scratched on their chests and shoulders and withers and rumps, but it took a veterinarian to show me about adults. I had a mare who was hospitalized, and when I visited her, the vet showed me where the mare enjoyed being scratched. It was a revelation to me; I'd had her for four years and had never figured that out.

Going beyond affection, though, I was pondering how much it's possible to communicate reassurance via the sense of touch. When Lily got concerned, it was an opportunity for me to put this idea to the test. I did more today when we rode again. Parelli Natural Horsemanship includes a game called 'Friendly' that is about, in part, confidence-building and the sense of touch. I have always approached it from a desensitization perspective, but now I look at it anew, as a tool for reassurance.

When I work in harness, I'm aware that my presence on the lines means something to my ponies. When someone else takes the lines, my ponies are not the same as they are with me. I had never thought about it as reassurance, but I suppose it is.

Like with the vet in the hospital, I feel like the discussion I read was a revelation: touching is about more than affection or direction. It can also include reassurance. I appreciated the opportunity Lily gave me to explore this new-to-me idea.

In the Horseman's Jingle, there was a 'Can You' called 'Can You Move the Feet with the Snap?' Before I looked at the instructional video, I thought 'This is going to be a piece of cake!' All of my ponies are taught to lead with feel rather than being tugged on. I use rope halters with heavy snaps on the leads, and when the snap moves, it puts pressure on the halters that the ponies learn to associate with moving their feet. When I got to the instructional video, though, I smiled. There was more to this than the words implied!

I have read often the reminder that horses can feel a single fly alight on their flank; they are very sensitive. Pat Parelli makes the distinction between touching the air, the hair, the skin, and the muscles. This 'Can You' was about seeing just how light you can be with movement of the snap before you get a reaction. When do they feel you making contact? Is it before you feel the contact?

What an incredibly humbling experience. As one of my Jingle friends said after she tried it, "I'm such a brute!" The ponies can feel the slightest movement, yet so often I use way more than that to communicate with them. I'm essentially shouting at them through their sense of touch. With my two work ponies who are the most responsive to me, it took hardly any deflection of the snap at all before they moved their feet, and that was using web halters (what I had handy) versus rope halters.

Next I decided to see how much shouting my stallion Apollo was accustomed to. When we first started, I had the snap way above horizontal and was tugging to get him to back up. Part of the problem was poor footing, part of it was having a mare standing in the way, and the rest was that we hadn't done anything like this in awhile. So the answer was that he needed me to shout before his feet moved. Within five minutes, though, you can see in the picture that the snap got just to horizontal. If I hadn't been focused on taking the picture, I'm sure we could have gotten at least to a 45 degree deflection as Apollo is usually pretty responsive.

This is the sort of exercise that I can play with no matter the weather. It's definitely given me a lot to think about. Just how much contact do I really need to use, whether through the snap or via a bit even? It's amazing to think what our relationship could be and what we could do if I could just 'whisper' at them all the time.

A DIFFERENT TAKE ON THE SQUEEZE GAME

The Squeeze Game is one of the seven games of Parelli Natural Horsemanship. I think of these 'games' as structured interactions that teach skills to both person and pony. This game is about confidence in tight spaces such as gates, trailers, and over jumps. In training sessions on the ground, I start out with a squeeze game between me and a fence, standing several yards back from the fence and gradually moving closer, making sure that the pony stays calm and confident going through the narrowing gap and turning to face on either side of me.

I took some of the ponies back to 'summer' pasture one November, and I learned a lot about how different it is in winter. From my perspective, other than the ground being mostly covered by snow, the biggest difference was that the Michigan River was partially covered with ice. I didn't think it was that big a deal, though, since I've seen one of my mares walk out on ice in other places. But I was wrong. The sound of the river water flowing against and through the ice, similar to swirling water and ice cubes in a glass, was of great concern to the ponies. It seemed as though the river that provided them water during the summer and that they crossed willingly on a regular basis had turned into some sort of menace. During the few hours that I had the ponies at pasture, they stayed as far away from it as they could.

Beauty and Rose, however, did venture closer. There is a fence that runs perpendicular to the river, with a gap of about ten feet along the river giving them access beyond to a small yard and shed. I left the pasture for an hour, and during that time Beauty and Rose had gone around the end of the fence into the shed yard. When I returned, I saw them there, and then I saw them exhibiting some very strange behavior. They would run along the shed side of the yard fence but then slam to a stop when they got close to the river and run back the other way. They wanted to come to me, but they were too afraid to go around the end of the fence near the river.

Their fear concerned me, so I started walking toward them. This caused them to charge the river a few more times and then retreat. Meanwhile, the rest of the ponies were watching them with concern since Beauty was the lead mare and was obviously upset. As I got to the fence I could see that my presence was calming them somewhat, and when I entered the yard, Rose came to say hello. Then I got to see the different version of the Squeeze Game. I stepped back and stood at the edge of the river, creating a gap of about eight feet between me and the end of the fence. Rose touched my outstretched hand then scooted around the end of the fence and ran to the rest of the herd. My presence between her and the river apparently gave her confidence to overcome her fear of the sounds behind me and enabled her escape from 'jail.' Beauty then approached me, touched my outstretched hand and then also scooted around the end of the fence and back to the rest of the herd.

I knew the Squeeze Game was about developing confidence in navigating tight spaces, but I'd never considered my role in the game other than as fence post and director. Beauty and Rose showed me that my presence can actually instill confidence. I'll never play the Squeeze Game quite the same way again now that I understand how great my role can be.

WANT VERSUS MAKE

Clinician Moses Woodson told this story once about one of his students. "She was asking and getting her horse to do the things that she wanted, but the way that her horse looked as it did them told me that the horse was not happy about doing the maneuvers. Helping her, we worked through her horse's attitude and when we ended the training session her horse looked more fluid and relaxed. It really doesn't matter what you can get your horse to do. What really matters is when you can get your horse to do an asked maneuver in a relaxed manner and get them to respond to your cues with softness."

I had been doing lots of groundwork with Lily (the photograph shows her at the end of a session hanging out with my husband.) She was fabulous in everything I ask her to do, except jump a barrel. I knew this already. Two years previously I asked her to jump the same barrel, and she refused. I eventually 'forced' her to jump it by applying lots of pressure behind her, but I knew she wasn't jumping for the right reason. She didn't 'want' to jump it for me; I knew she could jump it because she voluntarily jumped logs and other obstacles regularly for me. I was 'making' her jump the barrel. It took me two years to figure out how to turn the situation around, and she eventually started doing huge jumps over it voluntarily. We had progressed from 'make' to 'want.'

It is very important to me that my ponies 'want' to do things for me. It is important in part because they are my friends, and I want them to enjoy being with me and doing things for me. And in part it is because I use them for work, and the jobs we do are much more enjoyable if we are working in harmony rather than through coercion. And finally it is important to me because I think it leads to a safer experience for all of us.

I experienced that final benefit of safety when I took Lily on a short pack trip for work. We hadn't done any packing in a year, and I took the time to ensure that Lily wanted to go. I gave her the opportunity to sniff the pack saddle and pad and then the panniers, and I didn't put the tack on her until she had accepted the idea. The way that she communicated this to me was that she lipped the tack after sniffing it. If she just sniffed it, I knew she wasn't ready yet. And if she turned her head away without even sniffing, I knew she was not even close to ready. I stepped away and waited a few moments before approaching again and giving her the opportunity to indicate her desire to participate willingly.

On that particular day, I was very thankful that I had taken the time to get Lily to 'want' to go. After she'd indicated her acceptance of the pack saddle, I placed it on her back. Then I bent down, reaching under her for the girth. Without warning a loud explosion like a gunshot interrupted an otherwise quiet afternoon. Lily didn't even flinch, which was good since I was in a very vulnerable position at the time. Compared to Lily, I was quite disturbed that someone had shot at us. After a few deep breaths I was able to assess the situation and realized that what had really happened was that the tire on my 25-five-year-old wheelbarrow had exploded in the hot sun.

We then left on our hike, and Lily willingly traversed very difficult ground conditions. We traveled through a forested area with lots of ground litter that we stepped on, over, and around for nearly two hours, making lots of noise as brush and dead branches cracked and broke under our feet.   I was exhausted when we got back home. Lily was the same relaxed pony at the end as she was at the beginning.   I know that taking the time to get Lily to 'want' to go with me made our trip a safe and enjoyable one.

It is very easy for me to get narrowly focused on a goal and not pay attention to how my ponies feel about reaching that goal with me. More so than any other equine that has crossed my path, Lily makes me pay for losing focus on our relationship. I 'make' her do things at my own peril: I have been bucked off, run over, left behind, and knocked down enough to know that Lily's life purpose is to teach me to put the relationship first and focus on 'want' versus 'make.' When I put the relationship first, Lily is fabulous. I appreciate all the lessons Lily has given me about putting our relationship first and focusing on want versus make.

PASSING ON NERVES

I heard a story once about a horse that had continual health problems despite being on a very good nutritional program. I was told that the owner was a chronic worrier and was adversely impacting her horse's health with her worrying. I found it hard to believe.

A common piece of advice in teamster circles is to not work horses when you're having a bad day because the horses pick up on the teamster's attitude. I once read about a man and his team who took out several fence posts because he didn't heed that advice. My working ponies are pretty forgiving, but I still try to not work them when I'm not in the right frame of mind.

A study in Sweden confirmed that nervous people can make their horses nervous. Published in *The Veterinary Journal* in July 2009, the study tested both hand-walking and riding. In both cases, horse/human pairs navigated a prescribed course four times. On the fourth pass, the humans were told that a researcher would open an umbrella abruptly. Heart rate monitors collected data on both horses and humans. Horse heart rates followed those of their humans, including a significant increase on the pass when the umbrella was to be opened (it never was.) '…the horses responded to unconscious physical changes that accompanied shifts in the handler's emotions.' (1) Study author Linda Keeling expected the results from the ridden portion of the tests but was surprised by the similar results in the hand portion, since there was not direct physical contact between horse and human.

This study finally made a believer out of me about that worrier-owned horse and reinforced that teamster wisdom. It has also made me ponder how I might be impacting my ponies that I'm not aware of. I know some of the ponies come to console me when I'm upset, and one pony in particular mirrors how I'm feeling about life to a disconcerting degree. I am continually amazed by how much depth these ponies add to my life.

(1) *Equus*, Sept. 2009, volume 384, p. 16

NATURAL HORSEMANSHIP WITH ... DUCKS?!

The emphasis during one phase in my natural horsemanship studies was using the smallest possible cue when asking a pony for something. When I watch videos of other students, it's easy for me to see excessive hand waving or movement of feet in the case of ground work, or heavy-handedness on reins in the case of riding. It's a much different situation, however, to catch myself in the act when I am guilty of similar excessiveness.

I was laughing one day while doing chores about how another species in my barnyard population has helped me minimize my actions. In addition to ponies, I have stewarded a flock of ducks. I let the ducks out when I'm doing chores so they can graze on any sprouting greenery in the yard (they are penned the rest of the day to protect them from our numerous predators). Ducks are easily herded, which is why they are a favorite training tool for herding dogs.

The ducks give me excellent feedback about my movements, whether it's walking towards them (they raise their heads and focus their attention on me), lifting an arm (they move away from it slowly), and both (they move away more quickly). If I move slowly and subtly, they walk in front of me calmly. If I am faster or more aggressive, they spread their wings (my ducks don't fly, as they are too heavy-bodied). They will vocalize if I'm using more pressure than they are comfortable with. I don't realize how subtly I move around my ducks until I have visitors and watch how the ducks respond to them.

A true test of my subtlety was my Muscovy hen. She had the ability to raise the feathers on the back of her head into a crest when she was feeling stress, followed by a squawking vocalization. She also was wilier than the other ducks, resisting subtle clues about direction if the fancy struck her. I consider her the pony or mule of the duck family in terms of her intelligence and occasional intransigence. She taught me a lot.

In conclusion, if you need help minimizing your actions in working with ponies, I highly recommend a flock of ducks as a training aid. An added bonus is that there's no happier barnyard critter to be found!

LESSONS FROM PONY HUGS

"[A] dog will do virtually anything for a hug. A horse will do virtually nothing for a hug." (1)

So says Joe Camp in his book *Soul of a Horse*. Generally I agree with Camp. I have rarely had a pony do anything to attract physical displays of affection. My mare Matty is the one exception that I have experienced.

Matty will approach my husband or me, and while we are focused on greeting her with a rub on her face or a stroke on her neck or a scratch on the point of her shoulder, it will seem like she's walking right past us. She stops, though, just as her back reaches us. We have learned from scratching her withers and having her move to a similar position that she really wants her back scratched. She has repositioned my buck and rail fence numerous times by walking under the top rail to achieve the same end.

As she has matured and filled out, Matty's pointed positioning for physical attention has become a little more annoying. Like a good traditional Fell Pony, her torso has broadened out so that she passes me with her shoulder but bumps me with her ribs. This behavior brings to mind the fullness of Camp's quote: "[A] dog will do virtually anything for a hug. A horse will do virtually nothing for a hug. But he will do virtually anything for his respected leader. And he will continually test that leader to see if he or she is still worthy of the title." (2)

I consider Matty's choice of position, including bumping me, to be a test of me as a leader. The reality is that she isn't asking for physical displays of affection like hugs. Instead, she's asking for me to do as another pony

154

would do. She and her daughter Libby regularly scratch each other's toplines. By asking me to scratch her in her favorite place, Matty is offering me entry to her herd, which I appreciate, as it's better than being excluded. However, by letting Matty approach how she likes and invade my space by bumping me, I've effectively let Matty be the leader of our herd of two, failing the leadership test in Matty's mind. Matty is presenting me with yet another opportunity to improve my horsemanship; it's a good thing I enjoy being a perpetual student!

---

(1)   Camp, Joe. *The Soul of a Horse: Life Lessons from the Herd.* New York, Harmony Books, 2008, p. 40

(2)   Same as #1.

TESTING TEMPERAMENT

An article appeared in the Summer 2007 issue of *The Fjord Herald* about testing the temperament of equines. (1) (*The Fjord Herald* is the newsletter of the Norwegian Fjord Horse Registry.) The article summarized a study done by the French National Institute for Agricultural Research. Nine tests were developed to assess the temperament of equines eight months and older. The tests included opening an umbrella in front of a foal and watching how far the foal retreats and putting a sheet on the ground between a foal and its dinner and watching whether the foal goes over or around the sheet. While acknowledging that age, gender, and genetics influence behavioral development, the tests still led to the identification of two distinct personality types. The first was more fearful but more successful over jumps and at dressage. The second was less fearful and less reactive and more likely to be a safe choice for leisure riding.

The author pointed out that having a basic understanding of an individual equine's personality type leads to a safer relationship between horse and rider. She also pointed out that targeting an individual equine into activities consistent with its personality type would go a long way to ensuring the equine a useful and happy life. She framed her discussion with a story about a client looking for a dead-broke horse. "I found myself wondering how many people had two such horses, 'One for pride, one for ride,; the auto equivalency of a sports car versus a reliable SUV." (2)

Within my pony herd, I have had a few SUVs and a few that tend more toward the sports car end of the spectrum. There is no question that the sports cars are flashy movers and the SUVs I choose when safety is paramount. It seems to me that there are shades of gray in between, but I agree with the overall message: taking a pony's temperament into account when assigning it tasks to do is likely to ensure success and happiness for all concerned.

---

1. Bushnell, Ruth. "[The Test of] Temperament," *Fjord Herald*, Summer 2007, Norwegian Fjord Horse Registry, p. 12-14.
2. Bushnell, p. 12.

RIGHT MIND, RIGHT BODY

In 2011, I read a very insightful commentary on working ponies. Janet McNally, a Norwegian Fjord Horse breeder, characterized the ideal working equine as one who has the right body and the right mind. She defined right body as "wide in the chest, lower center of gravity and powerful hind quarters." She defined right mind as having "a great work ethic, are not overly sensitive, they can be rock solid when properly trained, and are never inclined to kick out behind." (1) While I have thought extensively about these things, I have never been able to distill the ideas down to such a simple description as McNally has done.

McNally then described four of the Norwegian Fjord Horses she has bred. Only two have both the right mind and the right body. Another has the right mind but a less than ideal body (too tall and slender), and the last has neither. This mare is for sale as a riding horse. I especially appreciated McNally's assessment of the mare: "it's not that she could not be trained to work in harness, but just that life is so much easier when these things just come naturally." (2)

Applying the terms 'right mind' and 'right body' to my work ponies, I would say that Mya has the 'right mind' but lacks the 'right body,' since she is light in bone. My Norwegian Fjord Horse gelding Torrin, my second pony, has the 'right body,' and while his mind isn't as good as Mya's, it's close enough to make him a good work animal. These two left me with the impression that all ponies have minds appropriate for work. Boy, was I naive. Despite the working heritage of both the Norwegian Fjord Horse and the British native pony breeds, not all individuals of these breeds are necessarily good work animals.

In the last few years I have experimented with working several Fjords and Fells in harness. In both breeds, I have discovered firsthand what McNally has found in Fjord horses; that not all of them necessarily have the 'right mind' and the 'right body.'

Early in my journey with working ponies, I felt that the 'right body' was elusive, but I then found the 'right mind' to be even more so. I've been pondering why, and the most obvious answer is that so few people work ponies in harness that they don't know how to select for the 'right mind' when breeding. I've also concluded that having the 'right mind' is more important in draft work than any of the other uses to which a pony can be put. It seems to me that there is a spectrum of uses, from pasture ornament to human companion to riding, packing, driving, and then draft work. I have personal experience with each of these uses, and I have found that along that spectrum of uses, there is an increasing element of risk involved. For instance, there is a much greater risk of injury, to horse or human, driving a cart than interacting with a pony over a fence. And there is a greater risk of injury pulling a mower with its sharp blades than taking a trail ride. McNally acknowledges that riding requires less of a 'right mind' than draft work when she says that her mare lacking in the mind department is more suited to ridden work.

Since riding is the predominant use of ponies these days, it makes sense that the mind needed for driving or draft work isn't important to most people or even understood. Yet for me, the 'right mind' is even more critical than the 'right body.' I interviewed Doc Hammill, a nationally known working horsemanship instructor, and he asserted that we tax the minds of our equines in the work we do far more than we do their bodies, reinforcing for me the importance of the 'right mind.' I have personally found that I am more likely to work the pony with the 'right mind' than I am the others because, as McNally observes, it's just so much easier. And in my mind, safety for both horse and human depends more on the 'right mind' than it does on the 'right body.'

McNally makes a good point when she says, "it's not that she could not be trained to work in harness." I have studied the work of a number of master teamsters, and I know they have the skills to put any animal in harness and to work it safely. Most people, however, myself included, are not masters. For us, having the 'right mind' in our equine working partner is much more important. I have put animals in harness that don't have the right mind, when I still naively believed that all ponies are naturally good working animals. It was more stressful than enjoyable. I really resonated with McNally's conclusion, "life is so much easier when these things just come naturally."

---

(1)   JWN (Janet W. McNally). www.ruralheritage.com/front_porch/index.htm, response to "working Fjord horses," 2011-04-11 20:59:10.

(2)   Same as #1.

158

CONNECTING HOOF TRIMMING AND PERFORMANCE

Because of my interest in using my ponies for my work, I pay a lot of attention to every aspect of their physical well-being that I can. For them to be able to work for me, they must be physically up to it; I don't want to keep a client waiting because of a health issue in my draft animals. Perhaps it's because of my own history wearing high heeled shoes and then suffering back problems as a result that I'm particularly aware of hoof care and its impact on mobility. (I now wear flats exclusively, though when I was much younger I remember feeling particularly smug about walking the length of the Mall in Washington DC in three inch heels!)

Several years ago we took a course where we evaluated the musculo-skeletal health of horses by observing their movement. We got to observe a number of horses who had been trimmed and/or shod by a number of different farriers. A few of the horses were being used for barrel racing and eventing while others were being used for pleasure riding. I was surprised how much the hoof care varied. In some cases toes were long, in others toes were different lengths. Whenever there was a trimming irregularity, there was related impact on movement. It was clear that not everyone pays attention to the connection between hoof care and performance.

Perhaps the irregularities in hoof care wouldn't have bothered me so much if they hadn't been done by professionals. But my own experience with farriers also illustrates that relying on 'professionals' isn't sufficient for ensuring that our friends' hooves are properly maintained. I once hired the only professional farrier in our county to trim a few of my ponies, and I was immediately sorry. He lamed one of my work ponies ten days before a job, and it was touch-and-go whether my pony would be able to perform. This farrier had a belief about proper hoof angle that had nothing to do with the particular pony's conformation. Obviously that farrier has never been invited back. One other farrier didn't like horses, and he was never invited back either. I had one farrier that did a great job, but when fuel prices skyrocketed, he decided that I lived too far away. I took over trimming out of necessity. Fortunately Pat Burge's husband Dick had taught me the rudiments of proper trimming several years before. He told me at the time that it would be at least ten years before it made sense, and he was definitely right. I was pleased to be complimented on the trimming I'd given the ponies I took to the clinic. And I know I still have a lot to learn.

While it seems really obvious to me that toe length and hoof angle impact performance, I learned from the clinic and my own experience that not everyone sees the connection. So I was pleased to read about some research that affirmed the connection. An observational study was done on seventy-seven horses. An objective measure of 'long toes' was defined, and a correlation was conclusively established between long toes and pain in the gluteal muscles. Dr. Richard A. Mansmann led the study from his joint positions at a private clinic and at the North Carolina State University College of Veterinary Medicine. "Excessive toe length in the hind feet might be accompanied by pain in the gluteal region," Mansmann wrote in the study. "Shortening the toe can alleviate this pain within days or weeks." Dr. Mansmann's team added that "in cases where the toe length or gluteal pain was adversely affecting the horse's comfort or function, one could also expect an improvement in the horse's gait and performance after remedial trimming or shoeing." (1)

It is great news that this study confirmed the connection between gluteal pain and toe length. The unfortunate part is that 50 out of 67 horses in the study (nearly 75%) showed signs of gluteal pain and needed remedial trimming. It's clear that just relying on one's farrier to do the right thing isn't enough to ensure our equine friends are getting proper hoof care. Owners need to at least ask questions of their farriers and preferably have some knowledge of what an appropriately trimmed hoof looks like. For the sake of comfort at a minimum and towards the goal of optimum performance, our equine friends deserve nothing less.

The picture shows me trimming Ellie's near-hind with four paddock-mates watching closely. I was terribly impressed that Ellie was as cooperative as she was given the close proximity of our lookers-on.

---

(1)   "Long Toes: A Pain in the Butt?," http://www.thehorse.com/ViewArticle.aspx?ID=18195

GRINDER TRIMMING

Early on, after I learned how hard it would be to find a decent farrier, I took lessons from Pat Burge's husband Dick to do the trimming myself. I found that during wet seasons, I did fine, but when the weather dried out, the hooves got so hard that I couldn't manage. Good hard hooves are one of the things that drew me to Fell Ponies and Norwegian Fjord Horses. They're a blessing most of the time, but a curse for a slight woman like me trying to trim.

I once found a farrier that trimmed naturally and could get through my entire herd in the time it took me to trim a single pony. I was ecstatic. Unfortunately, he decided that the cost of fuel was too high to come all the way to my farm. I began searching for another like-minded farrier and discovered that they all needed to add a fuel surcharge, which made the bill cost-prohibitive. One of them suggested I look into abrasive or grinder trimming as a solution to my dilemma.

Pioneered by Phil Morrare in California, this trimming technique utilizes a hand-held electric grinder to grind down a pony's hoof. (1) Desensitizing the pony to the sound and feel of the grinder is the biggest hurdle to its use. Here are some of the things I've learned about grinder trimming:

- the farrier that recommended grinder trimming to me said that he wished he'd learned of it sooner, as he would have been able to keep more of his profits. A grinding disk and a good rasp last about the same number of trims, but disks cost about $5.50 and a good rasp is over $20.
- try out the grinder before buying. I have very skinny wrists, and some brands of grinder twisted my wrists more than others or were weighted in a way that I couldn't handle them. I found a DeWalt worked best for me.
- I have not found a battery-operated grinder on the market up to the task of grinding hooves. I bought a battery-operated Makita, and it is helpful for desensitizing ponies to the sound and feel of a grinder but doesn't have enough power to do real trimming work.
- A disadvantage of grinder trimming generally, therefore, is that you must do the trimming near an electrical outlet. For me, this limits its usefulness, as in the summer when the ponies are at pasture, I have to transport them home to trim them. At other times of the year, I'm dragging electrical cords around, sometimes through mud or snow which can be dangerous.

- Safety: hoof trimming is a tough job, and having well-mannered ponies is crucial to safety. Grinder trimming introduces other safety issues such as flying chips (eye goggles required), lots of noise, and the potential for electrical shock if the electrical cord lies in water.
- As with any motorized device, jobs get done faster, but mistakes happen fast, too. It is easy to make a big mistake quickly with a grinder (taking off too much heel or quarter, making appropriate angle or balance difficult).
- My dogs dislike grinder trimming because there aren't any hoof pieces to chew on!

I am not completely sold on grinder trimming. There is something peaceful and satisfying about a relaxed pony holding its foot still for trimming and getting the trimming just right in a quiet setting, whether it be at home or at pasture.

---

1) You can find much more information about this technique at http://www.softouchnaturalhorsecare.com/

DESENSITIZING TO THE GRINDER

Grinders are noisy tools that throw chips and dust as well as blow air. When I acquired a grinder and began to use it, it was immediately obvious that the first ponies on which to try this new technique should be my working ponies who are accustomed to being around chain saws and machinery. I was gratified that none of the three gave more than an initial questioning look at this new practice. The next pony I chose to try, and the first Fell Pony, was Lily who also is accustomed to machinery. However, Lily would have nothing to do with me with the grinder in my hand. She pulled back on the lead rope to its full

length, nostrils flared and whites of her eyes showing. Now what was I going to do? Most of my herd is Fell Ponies, and if Lily had this reaction, I was crestfallen to think how the rest of the herd would react. The grinder is a dangerous tool if I should lose control of it or be knocked off balance by a scared pony (unfortunately I have scar tissue to prove it), so I realized I had a lot of work to do.

It took me quite awhile to figure out how to desensitize Lily to the grinder. I needed a strategy and I needed patience, keeping our relationship intact and keeping us both safe. I finally began by showing her the grinder without power, letting her smell it until she lost interest and then letting her mouth it. If she mouthed it, which to me showed acceptance, I rewarded her with a treat. Lily responds well to treats as incentive; others of my ponies just get mouthier if I give them treats, so they don't get them; I knew this incentive system would work with Lily but might not be transferable to the rest of the herd. When Lily was comfortable mouthing the grinder, I ended the desensitization session. The next day I repeated the previous session, and after she mouthed it and was rewarded, I stepped back about ten feet and turned the grinder on. She showed her previous fear response, so I backed up further until she relaxed a little then shut the grinder off. I then approached her with it turned off and got her to the point where she would mouth it again, then ended the session. Over the next several days I was able to gradually move closer, ending each session on a positive note. When she'd allow me to be close by, I 'airbrushed' her with the grinder's wake all over her body, including her belly and tail. It took a couple of sessions before airbrushing was okay with her then one day she let me touch the grinder briefly to a front hoof. Success. The key seemed to be approaching and retreating with the grinder, rewarding positive behavior, and not pushing her too hard too fast. Now I'm able to trim her hooves with the grinder regularly as long as I let her get comfortable with it each session and reward her for trying. The picture shows Lily getting her hooves trimmed with the grinder.

During the week or more that I was desensitizing Lily, I decided to see how Ellie would do with grinder trimming. In contrast to Lily, who'd been with me for seven years since her birth, Ellie had only been with me six months, but she looked to me for leadership and partnership much more than Lily did. It only took me two sessions before I could trim her hooves with the grinder. What a relief! Maybe there's hope for the rest of the herd (and me)!

TRIMMING TOOLS

My small body and limited muscles have made me a believer in good trimming tools. I just don't have the strength or stamina to make mediocre tools work effectively. Getting one pony trimmed in a day (a little more than an hour start to finish) is a major accomplishment for me. Fortunately, I've been given some good advice about trimming tools along the way that have helped me be more successful. The following three in particular have made a big difference for me.

- Hoof Jacks: One of the best things to come out of my experimentation with grinder trimming was learning about Hoof Jacks. More than a hoof stand, a Hoof Jack cradles the hoof with the sole up so that you don't have to hold the hoof between your legs. It is a much better solution ergonomically for the farrier as well as for the horse. There is also an attachment that mimics a conventional hoof stand for rounding the edges. The folks at the tack store where I bought my Hoof Jack said that Hoof Jacks have become very popular with farriers. My Hoof Jack was about $175, less than the price of a farrier visit to my herd.

- GE nippers: When I bought my first pony, I knew I needed hoof nippers. I had a set on-hand from when I owned llamas. Soon, though, I learned that a run-of-the-mill set of nippers wasn't up to my ponies' hooves. A friend said that GE nippers are well worth the investment, and he was right. Several farriers have been impressed that I have my own pair. I wouldn't do without them; they are sharp, resilient and reasonable to handle.

- Belotta rasps: When I started trimming, I bought a few Nicholson rasps. Then Pat's husband Dick said he'd split a bulk order of Belotta rasps with me. What a difference they made for me. Belottas are more expensive, but for me they are worth the money. They are sharper and stay sharp longer. And since I'm not very precise with my initial nipping (but getting better all the time), rasping is an important part of the trimming that I do.

A HOOF TRIMMER'S PERSPECTIVE

One week I was trimming Lily's hooves in very difficult circumstances. It was extremely muddy, and the insects were horrid. We went through a lot of fly spray, and my brush was constantly in use to clean as much debris off Lily's hooves as possible before touching my tools to them. I switched to a less aggressive rasp for filing because the moisture made Lily's hooves soft and I knew I could take too much too quickly if I wasn't careful. The whole session reminded me of something I've wondered about: how much impact does a hoof trimmer's perspective have on the quality of the trim?

I know from experience that beliefs about proper trimming impact a hoof trimmer's work. That farrier who lamed my work ponies did his trimming according to his beliefs about proper hoof angle rather than considering the animal in front of him. But I've also wondered whether our physical attributes as trimmers, such as eyesight, could have an impact. An experience with my husband and his chainsaw put this question in my mind. He had gotten a new pair of prescription safety glasses, and suddenly he couldn't cut the end of a log straight. It is a matter of professional pride for him as a logger to have log ends that look nice, and it quickly became apparent that there was something wrong with his new eyeglasses that was making him cut incorrectly.

While an article in *Equus* magazine didn't addressed my question about eyesight specifically, it did confirm that a hoof trimmer's perspective impacts the quality of the trim. A study at the Royal Veterinary College in England found that handed-ness, whether right or left, affected the trim. "…right-handed farriers tended to overtrim the inner wall of the left front hoof and the outer wall of the right front hoof." (1) The study found that the difference wasn't due to strength of one hand versus the other but instead it was due to brain neurology,

166

"...specifically each farrier's visuospatial awareness, which is used to judge the midpoint of an object." The study's author stressed that farriers are taught to self-correct potential imbalances, and the study didn't assess long term impacts of the effects of handedness on trimming. The author did acknowledge that further study is needed.

I hope someone follows up this study and explores other aspects of the hoof trimmer's perspective and its impact on trim quality. In the mean time, I will remain humble when it comes to trimming and try to assess proper balance in as many ways as I can to overcome any bias I might have that I'm not even aware of.

(1)   Barakat, Christine, and Mick McCluskey. "How handedness affects farriery work," *Equus*, Volume 405, June 2011, p. 14.

STEWARDING THE HOOVES OF HORSES

When I received my first lesson in trimming hooves, I was told it would take me ten years to feel proficient. Those ten years have come and gone, and a farrier clinic in 2012 reset the calendar once again. It's pretty clear that like everything having to do with working equines, hoof care is a lifelong study.

When I got serious about working equines in harness, I purposely chose breeds with good feet. I live a long way from anywhere, and I knew that blacksmithing was not something I wanted to learn. And the first pony I bought had relatively soft hooves, helping me recognize the importance of hard hooves early. So far my ponies have done well barefoot.

I would prefer to hire a farrier even to just trim my ponies' hooves. I'm not a very big person, so trimming hard feet, especially in the summer time when they're dry, is not easy for me. I'm also not very fast. I admired one farrier in particular who was able to get through my entire herd in two hours, when it takes me an hour just to do one set of four hooves.

I've been an athlete most of my life, so when I first ran across the mantra "No hoof, no horse," it made perfect sense to me immediately. Footwear was something I was constantly changing as I ran, skied, or did the many other physical activities that filled my life before ponies came along. My experience caring for my body as an athlete has informed the care I give my equine friends. In addition, since I work ponies, it has always seemed to me that I need to give them every advantage to convert their motion into work to compensate for their smaller size.

My experience as a breeder has also informed my perspective on hoof care. The Fell Pony breed contains in its breed standard a section on movement. It took me six years of study to understand what proper movement for this breed looks like. And now I can tell when a pony's hooves need trimming not just by looking at the hooves themselves but also at how the pony moves. Especially for those ponies whose hooves tend to get long in the toe easily, a pony can't move properly if their hooves aren't properly trimmed.

Another interesting benefit of being a breeder is getting to see the hooves of foals on a regular basis. Foals are intended to be able to get up and going very quickly after birth. Fell Ponies are known for their good feet, which farriers who've trimmed them confirm. Foals' feet at birth, at least in this breed, are probably as close to optimal for movement as is possible. I never fail to be amazed, despite having produced foals for more

168

than a decade, at how quickly and easily these youngsters are up and standing, then walking, then turning and spinning, then moving at full speed. As an owner as well as a teamster as well as a breed steward, making sure all my ponies have feet optimized for their lives, as those foals' feet are, seems hugely important.

Which takes me back to the reset I experienced at the farrier clinic. Just how do we know what optimum hoof care is? I've heard about comparisons to the pastern angle, about maximum heel heights of ½", about preferred toe angles, and mustang rolls of the front hoof edge. What is the ultimate goal of all these guides? The easy answer is that the hoof should adequately support the body above it in terms of weight bearing and in terms of movement. But how do we know if the hoof care we're providing our equine mates is achieving that? The farriers presenting at the clinic made a very good case for how to answer that question.

The farrier clinic was put on by the Equine Lameness Prevention Organization (ELPO). ELPO is a non-profit whose mission is "to provide hoof care and equine care guidelines that are based upon research and the practical experiences of successful equine care professionals from around the world."

The first thing on the clinic's agenda was a presentation by farrier Mike Sussex from Torrington, Wyoming on hoof distortions. I have seen flares and long toes and high heels, but I had never seen some of the extreme examples that were displayed. The presentation emphasized how important it is to recognize hoof distortions at their very earliest stages. "[Hoof] capsule distortion is proving to be a primary cause of most lower limb lameness issues like Navicular Syndrome, heel pain, contracted heels, impar ligament strain, suspensory ligament strain, ring bone and certain cases of laminitis and founder. As a horse owner, it is important for you to recognize subtle lameness issues or gait faults that can be early indications that hoof distortions may be present." (1) Since I had recently seen graphic videos of how movement impacts a horse's foot, including blood flow and hoof wall flexion, it made sense to me that

even the subtlest hoof distortions could have adverse consequences.

The farriers then demonstrated a hoof mapping technique that can identify if a hoof is distorted. The mapping technique accurately identifies the coffin bone's location based on external references. Knowing the location of the coffin bone, or distal phalanx, allows a farrier to achieve the primary goal of hoof care, "…to trim the hoof so that it provides support and stability to the distal phalanx and therefore the bone column, regardless of whether a horse is being shod or left barefoot." (2) Nothing like stating the obvious, but it had never occurred to me that this is and should be the goal of good hoof care: to trim the hoof to support the structure above it, both for weight bearing and for movement.

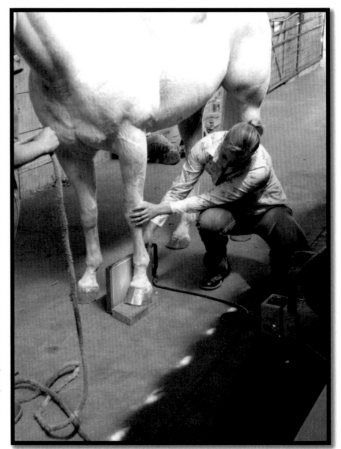

ELPO's literature points out that equines today are more subject to stresses to their feet than in the past. "Fifty years ago, many horses could get by without serious complications due to minor distortions and a little extra leverage because they were not asked to turn circles and do complicated maneuvers. Equines today do not have that luxury. Hoof distortions and excess leverage are a factor in the life of the modern day equine…. We have the technology to deal with excess leverage and strain, as long as the distortions can be recognized and eliminated." (3)

With the help of two local veterinarians with a portable radiograph, the ELPO farriers then demonstrated that their hoof map accurately locates the coffin bone. It was a profound moment to see a method that could be performed by someone like me with a high degree of accuracy and with integrity relative to the structure of the horse's limb. I expressed pleasure that as a horse owner I didn't need expensive x-rays to ascertain the location of the coffin bone, and the veterinarians jokingly expressed disappointment since it was cutting them out of a job!

I realized when I saw this demonstration that when I was trimming hooves, I was making assumptions about the relationship of the underlying bone structure to the hoof wall. I didn't really know if I was giving the bone structure support or not. And I am not alone. "Many farriers believe and were taught that the dorsal surface of the distal phalanx maintains a parallel relationship with the dorsal surface of the hoof wall…. However, the hoof capsule can easily be pulled, bent, shifted, and curled in ways that make this 'assumption' incorrect in many cases." (4)

So while the farrier clinic reset my calendar regarding feeling proficient at hoof trimming, it did have great benefit. Now at least I know where to put my efforts: either make lots of money to bring in an ELPO farrier or learn ELPO's hoof mapping technique so that I can trim my ponies hooves optimally relative to their underlying physical structure. Either way, I'll become a better steward of the hooves in my care.

1) "Recognizing Hoof Distortions: Tips for the Hoof Care Novice and Professional," Brochure, Equine Lameness Prevention Organization, www.e-hoofcare.com, undated.
2) "The Widest Part of the Foot: A Study of Locating Internal Hoof Structures from External References," brochure, Equine Lameness Prevention Organization, www.e-hoofcare.com, 2009.
3) Same as #2
4) Same as #2

HORSES... PREFER HAY

A Facebook 'friend' posted a status that brought a smile to my face. She had visited a doctor's office and was chagrined to see hay on the floor where she sat; it had fallen off her jacket. There was no question that I had to 'like' this post. On town runs I inevitably leave hay at the fuel company, the bank, the post office, and the auto parts store, basically anywhere I stand still for a few moments. Even when I 'dress up' for trips to the 'big city,' my chiropractor has been known to pick hay seeds out of my hair!

Cornell University did a study about horses and hay. The researchers devised an experiment to assess how much and whether horses prefer hay or pelleted feed rations. "...horses are willing to 'work' more to obtain hay when it's lacking from their diet than to obtain another source of fiber" such as pellets, the study concluded. (1) I find studies such as this fascinating. Knowing what I know about equine biology, hay and/or pasture are hugely important for equine health. So it makes sense to me that horses would prefer hay to pellets. It's only 'natural' for their biology. Researcher Jaime Elia, DVM, MS also pointed out that "Horses typically spend 65 percent of their time grazing, and when they spend only a fraction of that eating a pelleted diet, what do they do with the rest of their time?" The study found that they make up the time foraging for edibles in their bedding. Elia also said that vices such as cribbing or weaving could result. (2) This suggests to me that horses prefer hay not just physiologically but mentally and emotionally, too.

I know I'm not alone in having an ability to leave bits of hay wherever I go. I can understand the attraction of pelleted feed rations that wouldn't leave calling cards on my clothes. For the sake of the equines in my life,

172

though, I'll keep feeding hay. I'll endure the occasional bits of hay that appear in my bed and in my own meals, as well as the brisk sweeps of countertops at businesses after I leave!

(1)   Barakat, Christine, and Mick McCluskey, BVSc, MACVSc. "How much your horse wants his hay," *Equus*, February 2011, Issue 401, p. 15.

(2)   Barakat, p. 15.

FEEDING FOR TEMPERAMENT

I am a big believer in the importance of good nutrition for optimal health and performance. One collateral benefit of good nutrition for my ponies is calmer temperaments. While I've found by trial and error a few nutritional things that contribute to calmer ponies, I learned of one that I hadn't previously known. It turns out that supporting the gut bacteria facilitates serotonin production which can lead to calmer equines. Many things I do for overall health support the gut flora, so many of my feeding-for-temperament discoveries are probably related to serotonin production.

Minerals

One of the first things I discovered regarding feeding for temperament was the importance of minerals. Several years ago I had a stallion that one week seemed to develop a hotter temperament. I found that I had let his free choice minerals run out, and as soon as I replenished them, over the course of a few days, his normal temperament returned. Now I know that when I see a temperament change in a pony, if I haven't checked the status of the minerals in their shed lately, that's where I head first. The minerals that I use are formulated to maintain a healthy pH in the gut, which in turn supports healthy gut flora.

Vitamins

Another thing that I discovered many years ago was that some vitamin supplements can increase hotness compared to others. My first unintentional experiment was on ducklings; later I noticed the same thing on ponies. Since in my draft-oriented world, hotness is not helpful, you won't be surprised to hear that I've settled on a vitamin supplement that keeps my ponies mellower.

Digestible Energy

I began my adulthood equine journey by spending weekends with my pony-loving friend Pat Burge. She instilled in me how careful one must be about feeding grain to ponies because of the seeming ease with which they develop health problems when on feed that is too high in sugars. While she still fed grain to ponies, she did so carefully. I haven't ever felt comfortable feeding grain to ponies because veterinary assistance is too difficult for me to obtain if something goes wrong. Instead when hay isn't enough and digestible energy is required, I turn to a low-NSC feed.

NSC stands for non-structural carbohydrates. The term refers to the sugars and starches in feed that cause glycemic reactions in equines, reactions which can lead to colic and founder, among other diseases. Hay causes a very low glycemic reaction; oats, corn and barley create large swings. Keeping glycemic reactions low is part of maintaining calm temperaments in ponies, for as you've undoubtedly experienced personally, blood sugar swings are not conducive to a settled demeanor.

Tryptophan is a precursor to serotonin. The main ingredient in my low-NSC feed is soybeans, and "horse owners report that horses fed soy meal, which has about 5 times the level of Tryptophan as do oats, seem calmer and less aggressive than those fed oats."(1) Since I've not fed grain to my ponies, I can't comment directly, but it seems likely that comments I receive from visitors about my calm ponies are in part a result of my choice of digestible energy and other supplements.

Prebiotics/Probiotics
Prebiotics are a regular part of my nutritional program for my ponies.

The term probiotic is fairly common now, so what is a prebiotics? (Synbiotic products are also on the market.) Technically, 'probiotics' introduce live beneficial bacterial organisms into the equine digestive system. However, the digestive activities of the stomach can kill live organisms, so probiotic products must be specially designed to achieve the desired result of increasing the population of beneficial microbes in the hindgut. 'Prebiotics' get around the transit problem. Instead of introducing live organisms, they instead provide the ingredients for a healthy gut environment to stimulate the growth of bacterial colonies already in the hindgut. 'Synbiotics' are a combination of probiotics (live organisms) and prebiotics (nutrients for the health and reproduction of 'good bugs'). All of these preparations are heat sensitive, so care must be used in how they are stored and/or packaged. When I see feed products that say they contain probiotics, I always ask how the probiotic preparation has been protected from heat in the manufacturing process. If the product contains live beneficial organisms, I also question how those organisms are delivered to the hindgut where they are needed.

I regularly use some form of probiotic myself and have my dogs on them, too. Probiotics are especially important for equines because of a biochemical connection between their guts and their brain:

Serotonin is only used by the parts of the brain involved in a feeling of wellbeing and relaxation. It is important that there is enough for the horse to be calm and focused. But serotonin is used in far larger quantities as part of the "fight or flight" response in the gut. When stressed or excited your horse will produce serotonin that makes the gut contract to expel both blood (to make that blood available for the brain, muscles and lungs) and feces (to lower the total bodyweight to make fleeing faster). It is our belief that, in many stressed horses, so much tryptophan is consumed in the gut response there is inadequate left for brain function." (2)

The probiotic I use is specifically formulated to create a healthy gut that facilitates serotonin production, making it available for both gut and brain. It's nice to know that a good probiotic contributes to calmer temperaments in my herd.

Feeding Our Partners

Ponies often get a bad rap for their temperaments, and I think one contributing factor is the way they're fed. When we decide to partner with our ponies, inevitably I think we learn to feed them properly, too. When they're fed in a way that makes them calmer, they are more able to perform to their highest capacity, including using their smarts for the benefit of our partnership. And isn't that why we choose to partner with ponies in the first place?!

1)   http://home.bluemarble.net/~heartcom/tryptophantoserotonintomelatonin.html
2)   http://www.equifeast.com/English/Equifeast/ProductInformation/OptiMax

DOC HAMMILL ON MINERALS

Doc Hammill is a veterinarian, teacher, and teamster living in Montana. He is also an associate editor of *Small Farmer's Journal*. In the Fall 2007 issue, his regular column "Ask a Teamster" was about "Salt and Minerals for Horses." He opened his article with "In my opinion, salt and minerals are one of the most misunderstood and mismanaged aspects of equine nutrition." (1)

Doc Hammill then goes on to discuss the following about salt and minerals:

- Salt should contain trace minerals.
- Salt should be fed loose, not in blocks.
- Mineral mixes (especially the calcium/phosphorus ratio) should be based on what type of hay or pasture the horses have access to.
- Salt and mineral mixes should be provided free choice at all times.

I was thrilled to read these recommendations because they exactly mimic what I've found so helpful for my ponies. I use a free choice program with four different mineral blends. The salt contains trace minerals and is only available in loose form. Two mineral mixes are offered so equines can balance their systems based on the forage they are eating. And the salt and minerals are designed to be offered free choice at all times.

Doc Hammill concludes by saying, "With few exceptions, equines of all breeds and uses can be maintained in excellent health and condition on good quality forage (pasture and/or hay); simple, appropriate grains (such as whole oats); the salt/mineral mixture recommended here; and a good, clean source of water." (2) I have certainly found that the salt-and-mineral program I use is a terrific foundation for health. And it's always gratifying to hear a corroborating opinion from a vet and fellow teamster.

---

(1) Hammill, Doug, DVM. "Ask a Teamster," *Small Farmer's Journal*, Fall, Vol. 31, No. 4, page 22.
(2) Hammill, p. 22.

FOAL COLIC

What would you think if you saw a foal pawing incessantly in one part of the stall? In 2007, I saw Rose do just this at seven days old, and it was clear she was distressed. I'd never seen anything like it, so I called the vet. (It was, of course, after 9pm on a Saturday!) The vet asked me several questions, and it became clear that I was witnessing foal colic. Since the vet was two hours away, I realized what I needed to do immediately. I dosed Rose with my trusty prebiotic. She was better in the span of thirty minutes and had no further symptoms.

Also at seven days old, I noticed Rose's full brother Laddie flagging his tail and biting at his rear end. It looked like colic to me, so he got the prebiotics treatment and also showed no further symptoms. Since they are related, I suspect Rose and Laddie succumbed for similar reasons: eating hay (mimicking their mom) at too early an age, when their gastro-intestinal system wasn't ready to digest fiber. Perhaps there was some side effect from the onset of foal heat as well. I've never seen foal colic with any of my other foals out of different mares or by different stallions.

I dose foals with the prebiotics at a day old to ensure their gastro-intestinal tract gets a good start. And now I'm especially watchful at seven days as well. My prebiotic has also resolved symptoms of colic in older ponies, too, so I can't imagine ever being without it.

WHEN HAY ISN'T ENOUGH

For the first few years of owning ponies, I didn't realize how lucky I was to have such good grass hay. As fuel prices and labor costs have risen since then, hay makers here have gone to larger bales. In my mind this change has resulted in lower nutritional quality grass hay, though I haven't tested to confirm my suspicion. Despite my efforts to get the best grass hay I can find, hay now doesn't seem to be enough to get some of my ponies through the winter.

How do I tell when they need help? Sometimes it's because they don't have as much energy. Sometimes they lack a characteristic sparkle in their eyes. Sometimes they drop weight quickly during cold weather and then take longer to bounce back.

In the past when I've had difficulty putting weight on a pony or keeping weight on, beet pulp and alfalfa pellets (or alfalfa hay) have been recommended. I also know of people who feed a corn/oats/barley mixture, with or without added molasses. And others recommend a senior equine formula. While these products might be appropriate for more domesticated equine breeds, I'm concerned about how they affect more primitive equines, ponies in particular. Equines evolved to eat grasses, not grains, so their digestive tracts sometimes don't handle grains well. In the worst case, grains when incompletely digested can lead to colic or founder because of digestive system upset.

According to equine nutritionist Amy Gill, PhD, of Kentucky, "…people have grossly overfed horses for a long time; now we have a number of metabolic syndromes, Cushings disease, insulin resistant horses, foals that are insulin resistant, animals that are prone to obesity and laminitis. The big push now is away from starchy grains and to use more soluble fibers and fats…" (1)

I feel fortunate that I discovered a product that addresses my ponies' needs during the winter without the drawbacks of grain. The product is a fiber and fat source without starches and sugars. Just a few ounces can make a difference to a weanling, and a cup daily for my adults can help the sparkle come back into their eyes. Another advantage is that it doesn't make the ponies "hot" since it isn't based on grains. So when grass hay and vitamins and minerals aren't quite enough, I know where to turn to help my ponies with this difficult climate where we live.

1) http://equinechronicleonline.com/working-with-a-nutritionist/

NSC Value of Feeds

A few years ago, I went to a local feed store to inquire about digestible energy supplements suitable for ponies. The sales person pointed me to an article in *Equus* magazine about NSC values, a term with which I wasn't familiar. I tracked the article down in the April 2008 issue and found it very helpful.

NSC stands for non-structural carbohydrate and refers to the sugars and starches in feed that cause glycemic reactions in equines which can lead to colic and founder, among other diseases. Hay causes a very low glycemic reaction; oats, corn and barley create large swings. NSC values are a measure of the possible glycemic reaction. Typical sweet feeds have an NSC content of 67%, while the low-NSC products reviewed in the article ranged from 9 to 15 percent.(1) The products are designed to give the equine needing supplemental feed the energy they need without triggering a glycemic response. Typical ingredients include soybean hulls, wheat middlings, beet pulp, rice bran, and oil.

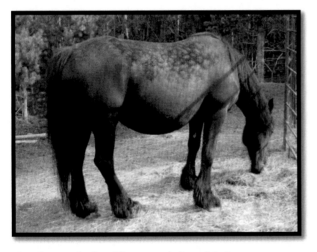

I inquired at the manufacturer about the NSC value of the energy feed I use. I was told it averages 17%, though it does vary some depending on the particular batch and the NSC value of the ingredients used. I appreciated this practical and honest answer. The ingredient list for my energy feed is what most struck me, though. Many of the typical ingredients listed in the *Equus* article are by-products of food processing. The manufacturer of my feed uses non-GMO whole extruded soybeans as the main ingredient, instead of hulls, retaining the oil in its natural form rather than adding it later in a refined form.

In the end, the *Equus* article said that management changes as well as feed changes are required to make the most of low NSC feed supplements. I know I have to feed this concentrate twice a day to those ponies who need it in significant quantities for it to have the most benefit. But I'm happy with the results, such as Beauty's dapples shown in this photo.

(1) Barakat, Christine. "Feeding to reduce laminitis risk," *Equus*, issue 367, p. 51.

Drylot Extras

When I started noticing the ponies not doing as well on my hay several years ago, I began adding things. Digestible energy was one of the first, and that certainly helped with their condition, especially their toplines, but there were other subtle signs that things could be better. With a herd of mostly black ponies, for instance, I was seeing the rusty tinges that indicated lack of copper when the ponies were off pasture during our long winters. Another symptom of copper deficiency is wood chewing which I had observed in my herd. I began supplementing copper, and it helped with the coat colors and wood chewing, but still things weren't quite right. So imagine my delight when deeply colored glossy coats started emerging after I started the herd on a supplement designed for equines on dry lots. Eureka!

Of course, hay normally has fewer nutrients than pasture. According to Juliet M. Getty, PhD, "Healthy, well-managed pastures supply your horse with many important nutrients, including vitamins E, A (as beta carotene), and C. Grasses are also high in omega-3 fatty acids in the proper proportion to omega-6s… Hay loses some of its vitamins and omega-3s in storage." (1)

The product I'm using that is designed for equines on dry lots contains vitamins E and C and omega-3 fatty acids, so the ponies are getting what hay lacks compared to pasture. The product also contains copper in the form that I found helped the blackness of the ponies' coats, as well as many other minerals. I have found dry lots indispensable for managing my easy keepers, so I'm thankful for a vitamin and mineral supplement that makes up for what hay lacks.

---

1) Getty, Juliet M. "Feeding for Immunity," thehorse.com, 12/3/12 at: http://www.thehorse.com/articles/30983/feeding-for-immunity?utm_source=Newsletter&utm_medium=nutrition&utm_campaign=09-09-2013

ARNICA 200C AND MY PONIES

I took a year-long course in homeopathy several years ago, and one of the last assignments was for the class to make remedies. At that time, Arnica 200c wasn't available locally, and it was considered a must in the class for first aid kits for acute pain following accidents. Shortly thereafter I was out hiking and turned my ankle. I took some Arnica 200c immediately and never had the swelling and pain that I expected after that sort of injury. I have kept this remedy in my foaling kit for years, giving each mare at least one dose post foaling to help with post-partum pain.

One week it was Laddie and Matty who benefited from Arnica Montana. Laddie broke into sweats about an hour after being castrated. I'd never seen this reaction to castration in any of my other new geldings before. The vet said that some colts are just more sensitive to pain than others. It made sense to me that Laddie's sweating was from pain. While the sweating stopped about six hours after surgery, it was clear he was still in serious pain, so I dosed him every few hours overnight with Arnica. It was amazing to see the difference in his eye after just one dose and then to see the gradual improvement over 24 hours. There was no need to continue it thereafter because he was obviously doing so much better.

One night my mare Matty gave me a scare. This normally voracious pony was not eating, she laid down in my presence and was groaning. Her symptoms reminded me immediately of post-partum pain, but she was five months out from foaling. However, she was just four days out from a cold-turkey weaning. After witnessing her pass manure and taking her temperature and finding it normal, I was able to rule out colic and infection (though I still dosed her with probiotics to be safe). I decided the cause of her distress must be pain from weaning. After two doses of Arnica 200c twenty minutes apart, her eye already showed relief. She also started yawning profusely and licking and chewing, which our massage instructors taught us are signs of release of tension. I dosed her every few hours during the night, and she was nearly back to her normal self the next morning (though still upset to be separated from the herd.)

Administering homeopathic pills to equines can be a bit of a challenge because in theory they're not supposed to come into contact with anything between container and mucous membranes. I've settled on a compromise. I take a small treat (about ½" thick by ¾" wide by 1" long) and spray it with a homeopathic spray. After tapping the container thirty times on my palm to activate the remedy, I tip several pills onto the treat and they stay in place because of the moisture. I then offer the treat to the pony (I haven't had one refuse yet!) The homeopathic spray may also have a beneficial effect, as its flower essences can address issues of pain and swelling.

Like all homeopathic remedies, Arnica Montana is effective in very particular circumstances. I have used it in colic cases, for instance, where it hasn't had the profound effect it had for Laddie and Matty. I keep it around, though, for those times when it can play an important role in caring for my ponies.

MASSAGE TO THE RESCUE

As a lifelong athlete, I know the importance of conditioning, warming up, cooling down, and taking care of myself the rest of the time to optimize my performance. I know what it's like to be properly prepared for an event at hand as well as the consequences when I'm not. In my many years of working ponies in harness, I've been successful using my own experience to prepare them for the jobs we've done. So I felt terrible once when one of my ponies refused to work because I hadn't properly prepared him. I was also a little panicked because we had a job to do a few weeks out where he needed to do some serious log-skidding.

I gave Torrin a few days rest then slowly brought him back into work. I've always assumed he likes our work because he reaches for the bit when I put the bridle in front of his head. He has only ever refused to work when he's hungry and he knows his herd-mates are eating without him (there are downsides to having intelligent equine partners!)

I had just brought Torrin in from pasture to work and he didn't reach for his bit, so I knew something was amiss. I checked for harness discomfort and problems with his bit without detecting anything. As I put him back to work he seemed uninterested in what we were doing, also very unlike him. As the date of our skidding job approached, I grew more concerned that he wouldn't be able to perform. I tried nutritional support, too, but he just wasn't recovering his joie-de-vivre. Then my husband suggested we give him a massage.

It was amazing. Torrin was subdued for most of it, very different from his normal, mouthy, exploring self. At the end we stepped back and he stood very still, also uncharacteristic. We just watched, knowing that massage causes releases of tension in unusual ways, as mild as snorting or licking and chewing or as active as stomping and lying and rolling. After several minutes, Torrin took a very deep slow breath, and it seemed his whole body expanded and contracted with his lungs. It was the most unusual release I'd ever seen, like a full body shake without the movement. Then Torrin started exploring his surroundings, putting his nose on anything we'd let him. I knew we'd done some good.

After two days rest to let him fully integrate the massage, I harnessed him. The moment of truth came when I went to put on the bridle. He reached for the bit! Massage to the rescue! Torrin successfully completed the skidding job that had had me panicked.

DEMANDING, I LIKE THAT!

Mya was demanding treats every time she saw me. "Demanding" may be too strong a word, since Mya is quite polite about it, standing a few feet back, tossing her head, and nickering. But for her that's pretty demonstrative, and I like it.

She had given me a scare when she wasn't interested in hay at last feeding. Here we go again, I thought. I was on tenterhooks for months after she got kicked in the head. Finally, after five months of close observation and decreasing amounts of treatment, I thought I finally had her cured. My heart sank then when it looked like she had relapsed. As it turned out, that night was easy compared to Friday morning. I got her interested in hay quite easily that first night, but the next day she only showed faint interest in eating at all.

At the time, I was working with my friend and colleague Doug "Doc" Hammill on an article for *Rural Heritage* magazine. When I talked to him that morning, I let him know I was distracted because of Mya's situation. He immediately began asking questions, and I remembered that while Doc is now a clinician teaching people to work their horses more naturally, his first career was as a veterinarian. Doc gave me pointers on using a stethoscope for diagnosis, but the most important thing he said came at the end. "Keep an open mind when you're next with her, Jenifer." He was cautioning me that I was assuming a relapse when instead I could be dealing with something new and different.

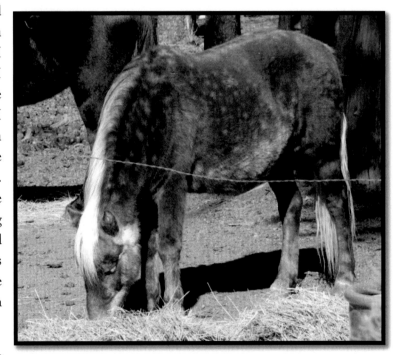

After we finished talking, I went out to see Mya and tried to put out of my mind what I thought was wrong. I realized from watching her with fresh eyes that she was in pain, though not necessarily the colicky variety since she'd been passing manure. So I treated her for pain, and within twenty minutes she was eating hay again. I treated her three more times during the next twenty hours, and she finally seemed back to normal.

When I talked to Doc next, he asked how Mya was. I told him she had an attitude, and he said, "Good!" I agreed. I'll take "demanding" over her being in pain any day.

ADJUSTING MYA'S ATLAS

One afternoon I gave Mya a massage. While she was much better after having been kicked in the head several months before, it seemed like she still wasn't holding her head quite right. The massage appeared to help, but after I'd finished I went back and gave her a chiropractic adjustment that seemed to make the biggest difference of all.

After I'd finished the massage, I realized that I'd forgotten to test Mya's lateral flexion (touching her nose to the girth area.) This is a common exercise in natural horsemanship to test a horse's willingness to give its head, so I forget that it's also useful to assess the alignment of the atlas and axis, the first and second vertebrae of the neck. Sure enough, Mya was fine on one side but very resistant on the second side. She was also sensitive to the touch on her poll. I sprayed homeopathic spray there that helps 'release' underlying tension. Her sensitivity was greatly reduced and she even seemed to enjoy me rubbing the spray in behind her

ears. She was also able to bend her head around on the second side, but she still did so at an angle that told me her atlas and axis weren't quite right.

When I received my certification in equine massage, one of my instructors seemed to be obsessed with adjusting horses' atlases. She showed us the technique, which involved putting the horse's head on your shoulder, clasping your hands across the poll, and then moving laterally and vertically in a coordinated fashion. It was immediately clear that this was easy for her and hard for most of the rest of us. First, she's tall enough that she can put most horses' heads on her shoulder and still reach across their polls and accomplish the necessary movements. And second, her mother was a chiropractor, so she grew up with an innate understanding of the underlying physiology of bodies, whether human or horse.

While it is second nature for Barb to do this particular chiropractic maneuver, I have to consult Dr. Daniel Kamen's book *The Well-Adjusted Horse* every time to figure out where I'm supposed to stand and how I'm supposed to move. I've even added my own notes to the book to quickly tell me what to do. I have another pony who benefits from this maneuver regularly.

I was happy to see Mya respond well to the massage and even happier when the homeopathic spray caused some improvement in her lateral flexion, but neither could hold up to the change in Mya after I adjusted her atlas. In addition to noticing that Mya wasn't holding her head quite right, I had had a vague sense that she was missing a brightness in her eye. She wasn't necessarily sick, but she wasn't right either. We've been best friends for years, so I've become quite accustomed to the looks she gives me, and they hadn't been normal.

Because the maneuver required for adjusting the atlas is so difficult for me, I pay close attention to how a pony responds after I complete the movement to be sure my efforts paid off. In the instant after I adjusted Mya's atlas, it seemed like her eyes flashed and then the brightness that I'd been missing returned. She immediately licked and chewed, confirming that I'd done some good. I observed her closely several times during the rest of the day, and it seemed like she was still brighter in the eye than she had been before. I understand even more Barb's obsession with adjusting an equine's atlas.

EQUINE METABOLIC SYNDROME

"Anyone who has owned a native pony will be familiar with its ability to create fat out of thin air."(1)

When I first decided to add an equine to my life, Pat took me to see a mustang mare who had foundered. I'll never forget the rocking motion that mare used to ease the pain of her feet. Pat had already impressed on me the importance of taking care when feeding ponies, and she'd shown me her daily management routine for her own ponies. The sight of that mustang, though, profoundly impressed upon me the importance of managing ponies properly to avoid subjecting them to the pain of laminitis.

That early pony health education prepared me well for stewarding my herd. Yet when I was asked twice about Equine Metabolic Syndrome (EMS), I was caught unprepared by this term that was new to me. Since the questions about EMS came from pony people, my pony health education obviously needed an update.

What is EMS?

"Too many horses eat too many groceries; it's that simple." (2)

EMS is characterized by three symptoms: 1) obesity or fat deposits in certain areas; 2) insulin resistance; and 3) laminitis. EMS has also been known in the past as peripheral Cushing's syndrome, pseudo-Cushing's syndrome, hypothyroidism, insulin resistance syndrome, omental Cushing's syndrome or central obesity. "A mysterious-sounding moniker evolved as well: syndrome X. Eventually, researchers agreed on the terminology proposed by the World Health Organization to designate this condition: equine metabolic syndrome." (3)

While the three symptoms listed above are common, there are equines that are diagnosed with EMS whose symptoms are so subtle as to be hard to diagnose. For instance, some are not noticeably overweight. Other

191

symptoms associated with EMS include frequent urination, lethargy and laziness, infertility or abnormal cycles in broodmares, sensitivity to touch in the flank and barrel, varying degrees of muscle tightness or even tying up.

EMS is often associated with equine breeds known to be easy-keepers. However, clinicians at the Unviersity of Tennessee have seen it in other breeds as well. "In our experience, this condition is most common in ponies, Morgans, Paso Finos, and Norwegian Fjords, but it also occurs in Arabians, Quarter Horses, American Saddlebreds, and Tennessee Walking Horses." (4)

EMS vs. Cushings

Many of the signs and symptoms of EMS are also associated with Cushings disease or PPID (pituitary pars intermedia dysfunction). What distinguishes EMS from Cushings is age of onset and how involved the endocrine glands are.

EMS typically affects younger horses and Cushings affects equines over fifteen years of age. Other distinguishing symptoms of Cushings include delayed shedding of the winter coat, increased drinking and urination, and skeletal muscle atrophy. (5)

From a clinical standpoint, EMS also differs from Cushings in that in EMS there is rarely anything wrong with the pituitary, adrenal, or thyroid glands. In Cushings, tests are conducted measuring the action of these glands.

The Symptom of Obesity

"According to research over the past six years, at least one in five and potentially one in two pleasure horses are overweight or obese…" (6)

While some EMS cases occur in equines with normal body condition, usually there is either general obesity or fat deposits in the crest of the neck, over the rump, at the shoulders, and in the sheath. If and when EMS progresses to Cushings, then there can be weight loss and muscle wasting.

Many of us may not realize what obesity looks like in our equines because we like them to look well fed. Here is a description that may be helpful: "A horse in moderate body condition will have enough fat cover that the ribs are easily felt but not visible. There should be enough fat cover on the withers, back, tailhead, pelvis, and shoulder so the body parts blend together smoothly." (7)

Studies have shown that many equines are indeed overweight and in danger of coming down with EMS. "Earlier this year a pilot study carried out by the UK's University of Nottingham's School of Veterinary Medicine and Science found that obesity rates among horses are as high as those among humans…. The researchers then assessed 15 randomly selected horses to compare their own [body condition] scores with the estimations of the owners. When the research team did the appropriate measuring for height, length, and girth, eight of the owners had underestimated weight…. 'There is a striking parallelism between humans and horses when it comes to obesity,' said Philip Johnson, professor of veterinary medicine and surgery at the University of Missouri-Columbia in a press release. 'Some of the very same problems humans encounter with obesity may also occur in horses.'" (8)

While it's easy to blame obesity on concentrates or supplemental feeds, it's also possible for equines to be overweight just on pasture or hay. In a Virginia Tech study, 51 percent of horses had a body condition score over 6, with 1 being emaciated and 8 or 9 being obese. The horses in this study were all pasture fed or fed on hay, with concentrated feed not part of their diet. (9)

Insulin Resistance

In one study, thirty two percent of horses with a body condition score of 8 or 9 (obese) had elevated levels of insulin. (10)

"Insulin resistance is a disturbance of glucose metabolism that can be thought of as an early form of type 2 diabetes mellitus. In humans, type 2 diabetes is more common in obese individuals, and high-sugar diets make the situation worse." (11) In the study referenced above in the UK about equine obesity, nine out of ten horses were fed some form of concentrated feed. Equine owners must be very careful to investigate the sugar content of concentrated equine feeds, as they can, just as human food can, contain hidden sources of sugars.

At the time of my research, there are two tests that can assess the presence of insulin resistance. The first, resting serum insulin concentration, works for moderate to severe cases. The other, combined glucose-insulin test (CGIT) is recommended for mild cases. (12)

Laminitis

"Although it is possible for an otherwise healthy horse to suddenly develop laminitis, it's rare…. More often, the horse has an undiagnosed endocrinological disorder…" (13)

"The most profound sign in most horses with metabolic syndrome is laminitis, and some horses will have several recurrent bouts." (14)

While laminitis may be the most common sign of EMS, it is not always easy to recognize. "An overwhelming clinical sign of Equine Metabolic Syndrome is laminitis, but not the disabling, painful disease related to gastrointestinal failure and endotoxemic insults. The laminitis exhibited by these obese, middle-aged horses tends to be mild. On occasion, so minimal are the laminitic episodes that knowledgeable, conscientious horse owners cannot vouch definitively for any clinical signs of lameness." (15)

While clinical signs of lameness may not be obvious, clinical examination will often turn up subtle clues of laminitis. "Abnormal hoof growth occurs. Dropped soles, unusual growth lines, and separation of the hoof at the white line are frequently observed. More damning, however, is the shifting of the coffin bone within the hoof capsule, which is obvious upon radiography." (16)

Thinking back to that poor mustang mare who had foundered, I knew that there was a connection to laminitis, but I couldn't have explained it to anyone. I was pleased, then, when I found this description of the connection by Dr. Beth Valentine:

"The words laminitis and founder are often, and incorrectly, used interchangeably. Chris Gregory, owner of Heartland Horseshoeing School and the virtual farrier at ruralheritage.com, offers this easily understood explanation of the difference: Laminitis is an inflammation of the laminae that connect the hoof wall to the coffin bone. Founder refers to sinking, as in "the ship foundered off the coast of New England." Damage to the laminae connecting the hoof to the underlying bone may or may not result in partial sinking (rotation) or total sinking of the coffin bone. All foundered horses have had laminitis, but not all horses with laminitis will founder." (17)

I once had a mare who suffered a bad injury. During her recovery, she developed a systemic infection, and the veterinarians asked me for permission to x-ray her feet because they were concerned about laminitis. I gave my permission and fortunately there was not evidence of coffin bone rotation, but I was very confused about why laminitis would result from the infection. At the time I took it at face value, which is just as well since the connection isn't even entirely understood in the medical community. Dealing with EMS is similar:

the connections between obesity, insulin resistance, and laminitis are recognized even though the mechanisms aren't understood. "The events that culminate in the inflammation of the soft tissue of the feet usually begin in the digestive tract or even the endocrine system... Indeed, to understand the causes and earliest physiologic processes of laminitis, you need to look at the entire horse, not just his hooves." (18)

A Prosperity Disease

"Equine Metabolic Syndrome is basically a 'prosperity disease' of horses that are genetically thrifty." (19)

EMS occurs where prosperity and genetic pre-disposition intersect. "An interesting feature of the disease is that in any given population of horses or ponies, certain individuals are susceptible to laminitis while others of the same breed, sex, and age managed in the same circumstances do not develop the disease." (20)

Two Fell Ponies illustrate how there is variation within a breed. My first Fell mare was estimated to be two hundred pounds overweight when a veterinarian examined her prior to my purchase. She never showed any symptoms of EMS in the fifteen years I owned her. In contrast is Janice's experience with her Fell mare. "My 16 year old Fell mare has recently been diagnosed with EMS following an insulin resistance test and a Cushings test (which was slightly abnormal at 29 but not identified as high enough to be Cushings.) It was recommended that she start on metformin tablets (14 twice a day) and she's been on them a couple of weeks now. I'm not sure there has been much change – her crest is still very hard and she is urinating quite frequently. Other than that, she is quite happy in herself – she's being hacked out regularly and is happy to do this. She's out in the field for 4 hours a day and in the stable with soaked hay for the rest." (21)

How Ponies are Different

Ponies are evolutionary marvels. – Dr. Amy Hayek (22)

"In the wild, ponies are programmed to put on weight during the relatively lush summer and autumn months, with fat (stores of energy) distributed around the body in preparation for leaner times. Significantly, fat is preferentially laid down in the abdomen, where it is known as omental fat...." (23)

Omental fat is thought to produce cortisol which acts to inhibit insulin and results in insulin resistance. "In relatively fat ponies entering the winter months, this insulin resistance has a physiological benefit. It preserves and prioritises glucose (and therefore energy) for essential areas such as the brain, at the expense of non-essential tissues like muscle. As the pony gradually loses weight during the winter, so the level of omental fat reduces and the state of insulin resistance becomes reversed. Eventually, spring arrives and the pony is in a

195

lean but healthy condition — ready to indulge safely in the pleasures of rich grazing. Unfortunately, this system has become unbalanced as a result of domestication. It has meant that the average equine diet is too rich and too plentiful. Grain-based feeds tend to be the main culprit, but even hay and other forages are now made from improved pastures and so have a high nutritional value." (24)

The bottom line, literally in the form of omental fat, and figuratively, is that insulin resistance in ponies and equines generally naturally fluctuates unless our management prevents it from happening. EMS can result when our management doesn't respect the natural cycles of the equine body.

Treatment

"Exercise is essential — not only does it encourage a loss in omental fat,
but it also promotes an increase in glucose uptake." (25)

A combination of diet changes and increased exercise is the most effective way to increase insulin sensitivity. (26)

As noted above, EMS can be difficult to detect if a horse isn't obviously fat and the laminitic symptoms are mild. EMS can also be difficult to treat because it primarily requires management changes related to diet and exercise. Specifically, treatment involves:

1) Reducing caloric intake
2) Eliminating feeds that contain starch or sugar
3) Increasing exercise
4) Limiting access to green grass and fresh forage.

Reducing calories can be achieved in a couple of ways. Calorie reduction can result from lowering the total amount fed, for instance. Or calories can be reduced by replacing high value feeds with lower value feeds, substituting straw for some hay for instance.

Eliminating feeds that contain starch or sugar requires first understanding where starch and sugar are found in equine feeds. They are commonly found in grain, for instance, so it is usually recommended that grains be eliminated from equine diets when EMS is a concern. If supplemental feed is required for increased energy, low NSC feeds are a safer source of energy for the metabolically challenged horse as they do not cause fluctuations in glucose or insulin level.

Starch and sugar can also be present in grasses. "Some varieties of pasture grass contain more sugar and starch than others, so contact your nearest Extension Horse Specialist for advice on pasture management for EMS horses."(27) "…many of the variables that influence the nutritional content of grass cannot be predicted or controlled… on a day-to-day basis, sugar and starch levels can fluctuate greatly…. This means that even in the morning plants may contain carbohydrate concentrations that could trigger laminitis in susceptible horses… If the owner is unable or reluctant to eliminate pasture access during correction of these problems, safety can be enhanced by utilizing grazing muzzles 24-7 or allowing grazing only in the early morning." (28) "Some severely affected horses may need to be kept off pasture altogether to avoid recurring problems with laminitis." (29)

"Exercise can be provided in numerous ways: riding, driving, ponying, round pen work, hand walking, longeing, or long-lining. Not only does exercise ward off obesity, research has shown that it improves insulin sensitivity in horses and ponies." (30)

Dry lots can be a valuable asset when it comes to treating EMS equines. If the dry lots are large enough, some ponies will exercise themselves by moving around the space. And of course dry lots are by definition free of vegetation, so the susceptible equine isn't able to ingest dangerous starches and sugars. Dry lots can be boring for some equines, though, so providing toys to play with can be an important part of a treatment plan for EMS.

In the discussion above about the Fell Pony mare diagnosed with EMS, the owner said that the drug metformin had been prescribed. According to a study written up in *Equus* magazine however, the owner's observations were confirmed that no change results from metformin administration: "…metformin may not be beneficial to horses with insulin resistance….The data revealed no significant change in the physical parameters in any of the ponies in response to metformin, nor was there an effect on glucose or insulin utilization…" (31)

Mineral Management

"a high quality vitamin/mineral supplement [is recommended]
as that is sometimes compromised when calories and/or starch is reduced. (32)

Because pony management often involves restricting feed intake, supplementing vitamins and minerals is likely necessary since enough of these nutrients may not be coming from feed. Supplementation is especially important when dealing with compromised health such as EMS. In addition to base-level supplementation, increased levels of magnesium and chromium are often recommended for EMS cases.

 "Magnesium levels in particular should be increased well over the needs of the average horse…. Magnesium relaxes the blood vessels for better circulation, especially important in the small blood vessels of the feet… Blood sugar stabilization and thyroid support are two other functions for which magnesium is invaluable. Magnesium deficiencies exhibit as nervousness, muscular tightness, irritability, excitability and poor memory retention. Most of the U.S. is deficient in magnesium in the soil, especially on both coasts and anywhere there is clay soil. The high stress lifestyle of many horses leads to an increased need for magnesium, and mares are notoriously deficient in magnesium due to estrogen levels. Since it is impossible to overdose magnesium and it is non-toxic, it makes sense to supplement generously, as the deficiency may even be a predisposing factor to the development of EMS." (33)

"Chromium helps the body to use insulin more effectively so that insulin and blood sugar levels do not rise abnormally. Anecdotally, we have seen reductions in neck crestiness and obesity with the addition of 1,000 mcg up to 3,000 mcg (1 to 3 mg) of chromium daily to the diet of an EMS horse, or even more if necessary. Chromium has the unique ability to balance blood glucose, as it lowers high blood glucose in diabetics and corrects low blood glucose in hypoglycemics. Low blood sugar is a leading cause of anxiety and nervousness, so chromium has stabilizing effects on the emotions as well. Building lean body mass and preventing the breakdown of muscle tissue in human athletes is another ability of chromium and this appears to translate into the maintenance of EMS horses as well." (34)

Prevention

"Ponies are [at] the highest risk, with breeds remaining most true to their ancestors, such as Shetlands, being at highest risk. Tough, hardy breeds like Icelandics and Mustangs, are also at risk, as are Morgans, Arabians, and often gaited horses." (35)

Since EMS is an easy-keeper disease, and most ponies are easy-keepers, preventive strategies are obviously of interest. Unfortunately, preventing excessive weight gain while necessary isn't a sufficient strategy to prevent EMS.(36) The same management measures for treatment – dietary and exercise – are necessary for prevention, too: decrease calories, eliminate starches and sugar, increase exercise and restrict access to green grass/forage.

As EMS is becoming better understood, new information is becoming available to refine management techniques for EMS equines. "According to recently published study results, feeding methods that slow horses' feed consumption rate can also reduce their insulin and glucose responses directly after the meal…" (37) Effective measures include putting obstacles such as balls in feed buckets to make it harder to eat quickly, or dividing feed into multiple buckets. When concentrates are needed, low NSC feed is also recommended, as is feeding smaller portions as many times a day as possible.

As we pony enthusiasts know, ponies are different from other equines. It turns out they are different metabolically, too, and therefore place different requirements on us as their partners. Managing their diets and exercise levels can prevent EMS and improve their overall health, helping them be the best partners for us they can be.

1)	http://barefoothoofcare.wordpress.com/articles/equine-metabolic-syndrome/
2)	http://hallwayfeeds.com/public/metasyndrome.pdf
3)	Same as #2.
4)	http://www.ivis.org/proceedings/aaep/2006/pdf/z9100106000051.pdf
5)	http://www.cvm.umn.edu/equinegenetics/ems/cushings/index.htm
6)	http://horsejournals.com/dangers-equine-obesity
7)	http://www.thehorse.com/articles/26055/feeding-broodmares-in-fall-and-winter?utm_source=Newsletter&utm_medium=nutrition&utm_campaign=09-09-2013
8)	Same as #6.
9)	Same as #6.
10)	Same as #6
11)	http://www.lloydinc.com/media/filer_private/2012/02/13/n_frankequinemetabolicsyndrome.pdf
12)	Same as #11.
13)	*Equus* magazine, volume 409, October, 2011, p. 14.
14)	http://naturalhoofcareofcolorado.com/files/Equine_Cushing.pdf
15)	Same as #2.
16)	Same as #2.
17)	Valentine, Beth,DVM. *Draft Horses: An Owner's Manual* as excerpted on Rural Heritage Facebook page 9/25/13.
18)	"Life after Founder," *Equus* volume 415, April, 2012, p. 37
19)	http://www.livestocktrail.uiuc.edu/horsenet/paperDisplay.cfm?ContentID=10118
20)	http://www.cvm.umn.edu/equinegenetics/ems/cushings/index.htm
21)	Same as #1
22)	Hayek, Amy, DVM. *Driving Digest* issue 185, September/October 2013,p. 19
23)	Same as #1

24)   Same as #1

25)   Same as #1

26)   Same as #2

27)   Same as #19

28)   *Equus* magazine, volume 413, February, 2012, p. 9

29)   Same as #19

30)   Same as #2

31)   *Equus* magazine, volume 406, July 2011, p. 12

32)   Same as #1

33)   "Equine Metabolic Syndrome," *Distributor Manual*, Dynamite Specialty Products, June 2013, p. 94

34)   Same as #33

35)   http://www.equisearch.com/uncategorized/manage-your-insulin-resistant-horse-h/

36)   Same as #35

37)   http://www.thehorse.com/articles/32178/feed-delivery-methods-effects-on-glucose-insulin-response

WHAT'S POWERFUL

It's noon, and I have fed all the paddocks but the largest. I'm about to crawl through the fence when the head mare sees me and begins walking purposefully in my direction with her ears pricked forward. When she reaches me, she accepts my initial pet on her neck but then turns sideways to the fence and tosses her head. The invitation to mount is obvious. Despite having no tack, I accept, and she carries me across the paddock to the hay yard.

COURTESY APRIL WHICKER

While I have these sorts of interactions with my ponies often, I still consider each of them powerful. When a pony makes a choice to engage with me and even better to offer something when they could choose otherwise leaves me feeling blessed to have such partners.

My ponies have made a lot of amazing work possible. They have also helped me learn what is practical about keeping them. The greatest rewards, though, often come in these other ways. On an average day I see more ponies than people. I have had the opportunity to learn not only that ponies think but that they enjoy human interactions. They want the mental stimulation we can provide. In return, they provide regular reminders that there is a lot more to life than completing a to-do list. You'll read several stories inspired by a life with ponies that look at life beyond the to-do list.

Sometimes, what's powerful is what my ponies teach me about myself. In the chapters that follow, you'll find stories about things I've discovered that I might not have had my ponies not helped me.

Ponies also provide reminders that there is a lot more to experience in the world when we use all of our senses. I've included several stories about watching my ponies be ponies, enjoying their world which in turn provides me with enjoyment.

Ponies communicate more through movement, such as the head mare walking to me, than vocalizations. There are a number of stories about my ponies communicating with me in similar situations. Of course life isn't always happy, and there are also some stories about lessons learned from trials that we've endured together.

Moon and Tug partnered with my friend Pat Burge around Lost Creek Ranch and out on the trail. Pat's Fell Pony stallion Dan, though, partnered in a different way. As you'll read in the first two stories, their performances before audiences reached people in ways that touched them deeply.

When my ponies make a choice to engage with me is when I experience the most powerful aspect of partnering. That's when I feel that one lifetime won't be enough.

Pat's Story about Danny

Orton Hall Danny brightened our lives everyday here in the valley. He was stunning to behold, fascinating in action, and awesome in expression. He came to us at eleven years of age and was brought to Colorado from England in his early years.

His beginning with us was slow and worrisome. He was fearful from the very first meeting, but, I felt it was because of lack of connection. When he was shown to me under saddle, he promptly reared, threw his owner and fled.

I was told he had been ridden and shown. I knew he had nothing to trust. Many symptoms of fear lasted over the years, but after some

COURTESY KITTY CURRIER

months, Dan began to trust Dick and I. He relaxed, he softened, and he looked for us each morning in the barn. Then he looked for us each afternoon to come back into the barn. When I came home in my little red car, he would race to the pasture gate, and run in circles as fast as he could possibly go, so I would notice him and come get him to go in his stall. Dan's stall was his security blanket. He would run into it often. In the winter he would gallop at breakneck speed from corral or pasture and nearly not make the corner to his beloved stall.

We worked in many ways, using much material from natural horsemanship methods to reassure Dan, and to train him to be touch-sensitive. I began at the early stages to work in the ring without any tack on his back or any restraints on his head. He would walk beside me or he would move ahead and come back. Obstacles were for him to go over, then wait. We went from ring work to the surrounding mountains and valleys. With time he became comfortable with many obstacles, strange animals, and strange noises. Interestingly enough, when his spooks unseated me, he was terrified to run away, so usually he stood next to me until I mounted and reassured him.

As Dan became bonded to us, he always added humorous little actions in greetings. In the morning, up would come the left front foot, and it would stay up until we got to the grain bin and poured some grain. If we did not get there soon enough, he would "ring" his grain dish, which had a wonderful bell-like sound, and he would continue to ring it until we got the grain. During all this time his ears kept moving forward. I worried at first that they might disappear from his head in anxiety. He would be panicky at feed time but also so comical.

Eventually Dan and I ventured out to a few local events. He did well as a beginner in dressage, and he loved to jump. In our ring with liberty training, Dan would jump over the jump, then turn around with excited eyes, jump back over, come to me and stop abruptly in front of me. Quite exciting to have eleven hundred pounds of pony in your space! That was his idea, and he was so proud. He always waited, and his eyes asked, what next? He was sure he had done the best feat ever and waited for me to cheer him on and find another great feat he could conquer. How could anyone ask for more when he gave so much? And with such bright eyes and delight! I chuckle now to think how wonderfully proud and pleased he was with how he had addressed the issue.

AT KENTUCKY HORSE PARK COURTESY KITTY CURRIER

As we met many who were attracted by Dan's presence, he became known as a unicorn. Eventually, a horn was crafted in a most unique way. Orton Hall Danny became Danequiel, in stories, poems, photographs, and in performance. In his own way, he became very dramatic, and many times he seemed to have a mystical presence. He breathed of times gone-by. He had the power and elegance to transform people into believing again in magic and beauty.

It was I that asked Dan to move into a different realm - that of giving to audiences, - and it was he that gave so much there, because people were attracted to him - and he could give them hope, beauty, excitement, magic - whatever they might have needed in an incomplete life. I asked for him to listen to me in different ways, and he was able to do it; through intuition we both connected.

As liberty training became so rewarding, and so fun, we began to add time in each performance to "being free". Dan was either at my side, moving dancelike with me, or around me in a large circle following my cues. I also mounted him bridleless and rode patterns. It was thrilling for both of us. He would respond to me as if it were a challenge and he could do whatever I asked. And now he seemed to accept an audience!

As I look back, I know we could have gone on with our partnership in so many ways. No matter if it would be home herding cattle, learning new "at liberty" maneuvers in the ring, or in a performance addressing an audience, he was always special. Some memories are so strong, he will be with us forever. For example:

- Dan often came in from the pasture to check on Dick and I - then checked to see if any barn doors were open so he could sneak in.
- While the Kentucky Derby photographer was getting some shots of him, Dan picked up Commanche, our 39" stud pony, gently, and laid him down on the grass. Commanche was furious, as he also was very proud. He promptly got up and bit a hole in Dan's rump
- Dan was so pleased to meet a young woman who loved animals, he welcomed her by rearing for her, and then proceeded nonstop to rear over and over in front of her.
- While practicing liberty work at a dressage barn, all the big horses were down at the far end, with their riders on their backs. Dan, at liberty, was trotting down to meet all the mares. He was a perfect gentleman, and they were all much taller than he and very snooty.
- Dan loved running into his stall and ringing his bell-dish.

COURTESY WENDY FRANCISCO

Thanks for all the memories, Dan. You are in our hearts.

Send us some dreams, Danequiel.

Don't walk behind me, I may not lead
Don't walk in front of me, I may not follow
Just walk beside me, and be my friend.
Albert Camus

A Unicorn grows in wisdom and grace
as the silvery filaments of his mane and and tail lengthen.
He bows his highborn head to no man,
and is fierce in his rejection,
yet is as gentle as moonlight
to his chosen lady.
from the poem "Danequiel" by Mary Jean Currier

COURTESY WENDY FRANCISCO

R.I.P. Orton Hall Danny

The first Fell Pony stallion I ever met was Orton Hall Danny. If I had known when I met him that I would someday need to keep not one but two Fell Pony stallions, I would probably have turned my back and walked away from the breed. At that meeting, Danny seemed larger than life and somewhat wild and fierce, reinforcing my belief that stallions were a handful that I had no business being involved with. Danny's display at the time was no doubt due to the ferocious windstorm that was gusting outside the metal barn in which he was housed. Fortunately for me I didn't know what I didn't know then, and fortunately for Danny, his life was soon to improve dramatically.

It has always been my opinion that the best thing that ever happened to Orton Hall Danny was being purchased by Patricia Burge. Not only was Pat a lifelong horsewoman, but she also approaches equines and all animals with a profound sense of compassion. That compassion led her to an ability to partner with Danny and help

COURTESY KITTY CURRIER

him to be the great equine ambassador that he became. When Pat called to tell me that Dan, as she called him, had passed away, I knew that a huge hole had been rent in her heart.

I never knew Danny very well personally, so mostly I experienced him through stories and photographs that Pat shared. It's clear from the photographs that Pat and Dan were extremely happy in each other's presence. Many of the photographs show Dan costumed as a unicorn. When Dan became Danequiel, wearing his horn, the two of them were truly in their element, performing for audiences. From Pat's stories, it's clear that, in return, audiences were captivated by these partners' display. While for me the partnership was about extraordinary horsemanship, for many it was about something more magical.

In some accounts, a unicorn is considered "an extremely wild woodland creature" that can only be tamed by someone who is good and pure and honest. (1) Additionally, as a symbol of Scotland, the unicorn is seen as "a proud and haughty beast which would rather die than be captured…." (2) In other accounts, unicorns are considered gateway animals to other worlds, helping us "imagine wonderful other ways of being." (3) To be able to tame a unicorn, to have a unicorn choose you to interact with, is to be recognized as being innately good and pure and honest, a form of recognition that is elusive in the real world. Often, according to Pat, Dan would interact with audience members in ways that left them profoundly moved, making unicorn magic a reality.

My first interaction with Danny squarely put him in the camp of "extremely wild woodland creature" and "haughty and would rather die than be captured." In real life from where I sit, Dan was tamed by a good and honest horsewoman, again making unicorn mythology a reality. I know Pat felt Dan was a blessing in her life. I'll always believe, though, that the bigger blessing was Dan having Pat in his life, for without her, Danequiel would never have existed, and this uniquely gifted pony would have been unknown in the world. Thank you, Pat, and rest in peace Orton Hall Danny.

---

1) https://en.wikipedia.org/wiki/Unicorn
2) Same as #1.
3) http://www.npr.org/2011/02/09/133600424/why-do-girls-love-horses-unicorns-and-dolphin

USING MY EXTRA TIME

One night I picked up *True Horsemanship by Feel*, Bill Dorrance's memoir about natural horsemanship. I have found the book to be best read as if listening to an elder statesman sitting on a straw bale outside a barn. Patience and good listening skills are required. The reward is that gems occasionally fall into my lap.

That night I was particularly struck by the following statement: "Thinking this way is going to take some extra time. It's really a question of how a person wants to spend the extra time they have." (1) He contrasts this with 'getting by,' letting things go, like a horse that won't stand still while being mounted, that could be solved and the relationship between horse and human improved in the process.

People occasionally ask how much time I spend taking care of my ponies. Some are surprised by my answer. Until I read this statement, it never occurred to me why I spend so much time on them. I realize now that it's how I like to use my extra time. It's never just about throwing them hay or putting on a halter or giving them vitamins; there is always an interaction to be considered, assessed, and learned from.

"Understanding a horse is something of an art… It's a sense about the horse's frame of mind and his thoughts about things. This part can't be learned from a book or videos. This ability can come only from experience…. Anyone with a sincere desire to achieve this connection with a horse could develop this ability. They need to have the time to devote to it and someone to help them once in awhile. The main source of information they'll rely on comes straight from the horse." (2)

Occasionally I will be asked how I learned to work ponies in harness since it's a long way from how I grew up and was schooled. While I found some books helpful and I got a few lessons from helpful people, my 'main source of information,' as Dorrance recommends, has been my ponies. Using my extra time to learn from them has had so many benefits that on a day when I use my extra time differently, there is a hollowness to that day compared to normal. Before long I'm back to spending my extra time with my ponies, renewing our connection and my learning process. I can't seem to do it differently!

---

(1)   Dorrance, Bill and Leslie Desmond. *True Horsemanship Through Feel*, Diamond Lu Productions, Novato, California, 1998, p. 24.
(2)   Dorrance, p. 8.

CHORE TIME

I usually enjoy my pony chores. It's a time to check in with each of my friends and observe herd interactions. I also believe that every time I'm with my ponies I have an opportunity for training. Chores especially provide chances for improving ground manners, whether I'm scooping manure, feeding hay or replenishing water or minerals. "No, you can't push your nose in my pocket. Yes, you will back away before getting your hay."

A friend told me she wanted to get down to owning one horse rather than being owned by eight. I can certainly understand her sentiment. Owning a number of equines definitely impacts one's lifestyle. Significant time, energy, and money go along with having these animals in our lives. Most of the time these things – time, energy, money - seem like limited resources that in turn put limits on the number it's possible to own.

In *Way of the Horse*, author Linda Kohanov. Describes the natural progression of things, especially with respect to the creative process. Somewhere between starting and ending there is inevitably a period of incubation, of not doing, to let the thing

COURTESY MARGI GREENE

move from the spark of an idea to a fully formed image that can be executed. Kohanov, rightfully so, observes that this incubation phase is rarely valued though it is highly necessary to the creative process, whether it's making a meal, writing a story, designing a home, or bringing forth new life (the period between conception and giving birth is of course a form of incubation). (1)

Kohanov observed that 'barn time' often serves as an incubation period for the things in her life. I know what she means. My chore time often bears fruit in unexpected ways. I progress writing projects, solve business problems, or have insights into complex situations that sitting still rarely affords me. I've never been attracted to the silent-sitting-still-type of meditation, but I often think of chore time as walking meditation.

211

In a story in *Savvy Times*, Linda Parelli wrote an article about a hard decision she had made. She had had to give up some chore time to get other things done. I've been told I should consider something similar to get more time for "important" things like training or managing employees or sleep. Linda shared in her article her angst about letting go of the feeding, watering, grooming, and conditioning tasks that she felt were a necessary part of her horse ownership. (2) I can definitely relate to that angst. Like Linda I would find it hard to believe that anyone could care for my beloved friends as well as I do. Linda proved in her article that that part at least can be resolved in an acceptable fashion. I would still feel angst, though, from loss of my walking meditation.

One night I was doing chores with my husband's grandson. I shared with him that chores are definitely a walk for me. I've calculated that I put in two miles a day on average. Yes, it keeps me physically fit, but it also helps me mentally; it is my incubation time. Losing any chore time, whether by reducing my herd or hiring help, would also mean losing that valuable time between spark and manifestation. It would be a loss I would have to carefully consider. So on days when chore time is a little more challenging because temperatures are well below freezing, I try to keep Mary Ann Kennedy's song 'Cleaning Stalls' in mind:

"It's kinda like a meditation
Sorta like yoga, it's my religion
I get in a trance-like state
As I pitch and as I rake…
All of life's problems seem so small …
when I'm cleanin' stalls." (3)

1) Kohanov, Linda. *Way of the Horse: equine archetypes for self-discovery: a book of exploration and 40 cards.* New World Library, Novato, California, 2007.
2) Parelli, Linda. "Linda's Journey – New Layers," *Savvy Times*, Issue 29, November 2010. Parelli Natural Horsemanship, Pagosa Springs, Colorado, p. 72.
3) Kennedy, Mary Ann. "Cleanin' Stalls," *Hoofbeats, Heartbeats, & Wings*, Tonka Records, Fairview, TN, 2005.

STAYING FIT FOR LIFE

A friend asked me how old I am, and when I said (at that time) I'd be turning fifty, she said, "Oh, Jenifer, you're starting the ten best years of your life!" I appreciated such a positive assessment of my future, especially since that year was setting itself up to be the most challenging year I'd ever had. And I thought the previous three were trials!

I always pay attention when items with similar messages present themselves to me in a short period of time. Four such items surfaced that had information about surviving difficult times. The subtext of each of them was that life isn't always easy and it's important that one stay fit – mentally, emotionally, as well as physically – to be able to capably face the challenges that inevitably come our way. I was of course heartened to see how ponies can play an important part in helping me stay fit for life.

The first item that came my way was an email from Teri Sprague, a Parelli Natural Horsemanship instructor. In it she told the following story: "I have experienced an interesting phenomenon this last year. Even though I have gone through some very trying times, it was easier than one might imagine given the situation.... Like so many of us, when 'life happens' it had been my practice to let my horses and my horsemanship go, in favor of trying to put these other urgent things at the highest priority.

This year, in spite of numerous difficult and long lasting challenges, I have logged more horse time than probably the last 4 or 5 years put together! As a result I have been more emotionally, mentally, and physically fit." (1) Teri concluded her story by asking why it was true that time with horses enables one to better handle life's challenges.

The second item of interest was a book I had finished reading. *My Stroke of Insight* is by Jill Bolte Taylor, PhD, and it gave me some insight into Teri's question. The book is about Dr. Taylor's experience of having a stroke and then her subsequent eight years of recovery. Dr. Taylor is a brain scientist and was able to analyze her brain's shutdown and subsequent recovery from her highly trained academic perspective. She summarizes her experience as losing her left brain, discovering her right brain and then healing to use her whole brain. "It appears that many of us struggle regularly with polar opposite characters holding court inside our heads… Many of us speak about how our head (left hemisphere) is telling us to do one thing while our heart (right hemisphere) is telling us to do the exact opposite." (2) Dr. Taylor also described the left brain as having a sense of self and separateness and the right brain having a sense of oneness with and connection to the entire universe. "Whatever language you use to describe [the two parts of your head], based upon my experience, I believe they stem anatomically from the two very distinct hemispheres inside your head." (3)

Prior to her stroke, Dr. Taylor's left hemisphere shaped who she was. "The judging and analytical character in my left mind dominated my personality." (4) The gift of her stroke was discovering the character of her right mind. "My right mind is all about the richness of this present moment. It is filled with gratitude for my life and everything and everyone in it." (5) In her recovery process, Dr. Taylor paid lots of attention to retaining the gifts of her right mind while rebuilding the analytical abilities of her left. "Creating a healthy balance between our two characters enables us the ability to remain cognitively flexible enough to welcome change (right hemisphere), and yet remain concrete enough to stay a path (left hemisphere.) Learning to value and utilize all of our cognitive gifts opens our lives up to the masterpiece of life we truly are." (6)

Many of the words Dr. Taylor uses in her book to characterize the right hemisphere of our brains are identical to ones that surface in natural horsemanship. She says that the right mind is "sensitive to nonverbal communication, empathic, and accurately decodes emotion… My right mind is ever present and gets lost in time." (7) The right brain does not have a sense of right and wrong; it accepts information as it is without judgment. To understand our equine partners, the ability to read nonverbal communication, to be in the moment, and to see behavior without judging it are all key to working with them as they are rather than as we think they should be. To answer Teri's question about why time with horses makes us more fit for life, the answer seems to be that it requires us to use our entire brain, not just one half. Time with horses requires us to utilize the circuitry of our right brains, circuitry which is often not honored or valued in our culture.

214

My favorite calendar was the source of another item about staying fit for life. In the same month that I finished reading Dr. Taylor's book, this quote appeared on my calendar: "Take time to find the stillness within. Whether it be through prayer, creativity, yoga, or jogging, devotion builds strength and graces you with a sense of peace and balance in body, mind and spirit." (8) I of course added time with equines to the list of activities that can bring a sense of peace and balance. The use of the word devotion brought me a new understanding of the term, as it reminded me of Dr. Taylor's emphasis on making the circuitry of our right mind more a part of our daily lives. As my life got more challenging, I occasionally did as Teri admitted, "when 'life happens' it had been my practice to let my horses and my horsemanship go..." During tough times, I found that it requires more focused effort – devotion -- to make time with my ponies important.

I was in contact with a number of people who work their ponies in harness. One of them was Libby Robinson in France. Libby was the source of the fourth item that reflected on staying fit for life. We were corresponding about the practice of using equines in our daily work, and Libby shared this sentiment: "Mankind has really lost so much of his soul now that the horse is not standing with him in his working life." (9) It seemed an appropriate summary of all I have learned about the role my ponies play in my being mentally, physically, and emotionally fit for all that life throws my way.

(1) Sprague, Teri. "Life is Better – From the Back of a Horse," *Parelli News from Licensed 4 Star Senior Instructor – Teri Sprague*, email dated March 1, 2010.
(2) Taylor, Jill Bolte, PhD. *My Stroke of Insight: A Brain Scientist's Personal Journey*. New York, Plume/Penguin Books, 2006, p. 141.
(3) Taylor, p. 141
(4) Taylor, p. 140.
(5) Taylor, p. 146
(6) Taylor, p. 145
(7) Taylor, p. 147
(8) Ministry of the Arts. Pathways to Peace: With Notes for the Journey, *2010 Calendar*. LaGrange Park, Illinois, March page.
(9) Robinson, Libby. "RE: Picture Story", email dated March 1, 2010.

Horses and the Pursuit of Happiness

While I originally got involved with ponies to get help with my work, friends have correctly observed that now I couldn't live without them, even if we never hauled manure or herded cattle or skid logs again. And I know I'm not alone in wanting these magnificent creatures in my life.

Some recent research about what leads to happiness provides insight, I think, into what can be a very expensive hobby. The link between money and happiness has been investigated often, but "very little research corroborates the idea that more money leads to more happiness." (1) If having horses in one's life provides happiness, then it is one example of the disconnect between money and happiness. My favorite economic rule is: The quickest way to make a million dollars with horses is to start with three million! Instead, how one spends their time correlates to happiness much more strongly than anything to do with money.

"If Money Doesn't Make You Happy, Consider Time" was published in the *Journal of Consumer Psychology*. The authors identified five time-spending happiness principles. Each of these, at least in my life, has strong connections to my involvement with equines.

1. <u>Spend time with those who make you happy</u>. My ponies definitely make me happy, and the amount of effort I put into caring for them looks crazy to outside observers but is soul-satisfying for me. The researchers recommend that time at work as well as other time should be with those who induce happy feelings, so it's no surprise, I guess, that I try to find as many ways as I can to integrate my ponies into my work life.

216

2. <u>Spend time on things that are energizing rather than draining and defeating.</u> "[People] need to reflect on how they are spending their time — the extent to which they mindlessly move from activity to activity without considering what they would really prefer to be doing." (1) Taking care of my ponies - feeding, collecting manure, and training - takes a significant amount of time, which I couldn't do if it wasn't enjoyable. Having the responsibility of caring for my four-hooved friends also means there's less time to waste on less meaningful activities.

3. <u>Day dream, study, and read about what makes you happy.</u> "Research in the field of neuroscience has shown that the part of the brain responsible for feeling pleasure … can be activated when merely thinking about something pleasurable." (1) Reading about ponies, studying working ponies, and being mentored in natural horsemanship training all occupy my time and have double benefits: inducing happy feelings at the time and fueling future activities that will likely induce happiness.

4. <u>Expand time by being in the moment.</u> "Unlike money, time is inherently scarce. No one gets more than 24 hours per day….. To increase happiness, it can make sense to focus on the here and now — because thinking about the present moment (vs. the future) has been found to slow down the perceived passage of time. Simply breathing more deeply can have similar effects." (1) There's no better way to be in the moment than to be with animals. When I am with my ponies, not only do they force me to be present by demanding my attention, but they also model living in the present. "[Focus] on the present moment, breathe more slowly, and spend the little time that you have in helpful and meaningful ways." (1) I was spending time with two-week-old Madie, working on things like leading and picking up her feet. I consciously slowed myself down so I didn't over-stimulate her, keeping her receptive to learning. It was amazing how much the two of us could do in very little time, but the time spent will serve her well for decades.

5. <u>Sources of happiness change over time.</u> "Recent research found that younger people are more likely to experience happiness as excitement, whereas older individuals are more likely to experience happiness as feeling peaceful." (1) Many young people I know are into high-adrenaline equine activities. Since I came to the horse world later in life, I take more pleasure in lower key pursuits. I often tell people that as a draft person, trotting is really exciting!

"[Although] the meaning of happiness may change, it does so in predictable patterns. Therefore, it is possible to anticipate such changes, and you should allow yourself to shift how you spend your time over the course of your life — as the meaning of happiness shifts." (1) I got involved with ponies to be active, and a dozen years later I am now often surprised by how much joy I take from caretaking and breeding rather than working. An older friend thought it was time to get rid of her pony and then realized that she just needed to figure out a different way to keep her. It will be interesting to see how my involvement with my ponies changes as I continue to grow older, but it's pretty clear they'll be in my life somehow, since they are so intimately tied to my happiness.

---

(1) http://www.gsb.stanford.edu/news/research/aaker_happiness_2011.html?utm_source=Knowledgebase&utm_medium=email&utm_campaign=April-11

Happiness, Hope, and Working Drafts

On yet another snowy morning here, I took hope from my friend Jim's email that spring was coming. A plowing match invitation had arrived for Jim, and he was looking forward to getting out with his six-Haflinger hitch once again. Jim spends most weekends during the good-weather-months taking his six to events. Mostly the events are about plowing, and he has developed a circle of friends that provide him with a phenomenal schedule. Jim claims they do it mostly for fun, but I know there are broader benefits beyond enjoyment and getting work done.

My husband was watching a TV show a few days before the Superbowl that was a contest between various Superbowl ads from the past. In the end, the first place commercial featured the Budweiser Clydesdales, and second place also featured these draft horses. Isn't it something that horses were featured in the top ads? Not artificial monsters, not high tech special effects, not human beings doing violent things, but flesh-and-blood horses? And isn't it something that it was draft horses?

About the same time, I read an article about a business school that is teaching its students how to incorporate happiness into the marketing of products and brands. "The idea of brands

enabling happiness and providing greater meaning in the world is powerful," says marketing professor Jennifer Aaker of the Stanford Graduate School of Business. "People have an aversion to anything that feels overly manufactured." (1) Maybe the success of the Budweiser Clydesdale ads is a triumph of marketing by creating a sense of happiness. I prefer, however, to look at it differently.

I also read an article about a young man who was drawn to the world of working horses by happiness and more, I believe, to do with hope. These words from the late draft and driving horse trainer Steve Bowers come to mind: "In this world that has been highly polluted in many ways with the machines of men, one sparkling glimmer of hope is the person who has useful work for horses, and knows how to train for that work with uncommon skill..." (2)

I think one of the things that people appreciate about the Budweiser ads and about watching draft horses in general is that they inspire hope: that there are ways to get things done that are more harmonious than the norm. And in these times, inspiring hope about the future is definitely a good thing. So when Jim's words about plowing arrived, and the hope of spring came to mind, I also thought of the bystanders that attend the plowing events at which Jim works his hitch. I would guess those bystanders aren't there for reasons of marketing; they are there for reasons of hope. They appreciate what Jim and the other teamsters are doing and how they are doing it. We as draft horse teamsters, above other types of horsemen, have an uncommon opportunity when with our horses. By putting them to useful work, and doing it well, we make the future look brighter for any and all that may be watching. And maybe we can attract more people to working with our draft equines, too!

1) http://www.fastcompany.com/magazine/153/the-business-of-happiness.html?page=0%2C0
2) Bowers, Steve. *A Teamster's View: More and Different*, Bowers Farm, Fort Collins, Colorado, p. 200.

RESPECTING THAT ANIMALS THINK

The cover story of the March 2008 *National Geographic* was "Inside Animal Minds." It summarized current research that debunks the myth that animals are incapable of thought or feeling. "Certain skills are considered key signs of higher mental abilities: good memory, a grasp of grammar and symbols, self-awareness, understanding others' motives, imitating others, and being creative." (1) The research has shown that we humans are not as unique as we once thought. "This is the larger lesson of animal cognition research: It humbles us. We are not alone in our ability to invent or plan or to contemplate ourselves – or even to plot or lie." (2)

The story introduced a parrot who could verbally describe differences in objects, a border collie who rivaled toddlers at learning vocabulary, an elephant that recognized itself in a mirror, and a jay who re-hid food after it saw another jay find the first hiding place.

When I bought my first pony, it was with the intention of having her as a workmate. Since I usually work alone, it's important from a safety standpoint that my workmate thinks through situations before reacting to them. When we encounter a bear on a trail ride or a snake across our path or there are guns being fired in the distance, I need my partner to make an appropriate and safe assessment of the situation.

Ponies often have a bad rap for being stubborn or willful or mean. I prefer the perspective that they are not machines or automatons but living, breathing and – especially – thinking beings, and they demand respect as such. No one should own a pony who is not willing to offer that respect. The result will likely be unfortunate, for one or the other or both.

While the *National Geographic* article didn't discuss equines, an article in *Savvy Times* discussed equine-facilitated psychotherapy. I found it expressed the sort of intelligence I've come to associate with equines. Here is an especially poignant excerpt:

"A boy stands in a field of horses. His assignment: to introduce himself to all four of the horses in the pasture in any way that feels comfortable. This is not the first equine assignment that the boy has been given. This assignment is part of his curriculum in the Horse Sense program Running with Mustangs, a youth development program for incarcerated youth who – aside from being delinquents – have been tagged as being involved or at risk of becoming involved in gang activity. The boy works his way into the herd and easily introduces himself to three of the horses but has problems connecting with the fourth. The remaining horse, Sugar, a Thoroughbred mare, came to Horse Sense as a starvation case. Her halter had grown into her head, as is common in many rescues. Her history left her timid, unconfident and very much an introvert. Sugar keeps another horse between herself and the boy. After several unsuccessful attempts, the session's facilitators pose a question to the boy: 'What is Sugar in your life?' The boy turns, looks at them and responds: 'Sugar is my heart. I'm not going to let anyone get close to that.' Immediately Sugar drops her guard, comes over to the boy and places her head on his heart. The session is over." (3)

(1) Morrell, Virginia. "Minds of their Own," *National Geographic*, March 2008, p. 42-43.
(2) Morrell, p. 53.
(3) Pugh, Terra N. "Horse Sense," *Savvy Times*, Issue 20, August 2008, p. 26.

DOUBLE DUTY STUDY

The other day when I was giving my pony Mya a massage, I was working one part of her body and then another, one side of her body then another. After about twenty minutes I realized that Mya hadn't given me any feedback on the massage. Then I realized that I hadn't given her any time to give me feedback. She has the sort of personality that needs time to express herself.

For the longest time my husband didn't bond with Mya. It was only after several months of being around her that he came to appreciate her quiet strength and undemonstrative ways. Immediately after I realized that I hadn't given Mya time

to give me feedback during the massage, I paused and stepped back. Only then did she take a deep breath and exhale and slowly lick and chew, releasing tension.

Later in the day, I sat down with an issue of *Savvy Times* and, in particular, an article entitled "What Does Your Horse Need?" The article breaks horses into different personalities and then talks about what each one needs to become the best horse they can be. For Mya's type, the advice felt strangely familiar. Mya's type "shuts down because he is fed up with being pushed or bored to pieces…. What to do is simple: wait. But waiting is not easy for us because we want the horse to do it now!... We see what we want and we go for it."(1) Guilty as charged! At least I caught myself in the act.

Between giving Mya her massage and reading the article, I had driven to pasture to check on the ponies. While riding in the truck, I heard an interview on the radio with a former FBI agent. He had successfully gotten intelligence about terrorism in an unconventional way: by developing rapport with an apprehended terrorist. He contrasted his rapport-building approach with the enhanced interrogation technique known as waterboarding. Waterboarding one apprehended terrorist led to intelligence that Saddam Hussein had weapons of mass destruction, which of course later turned out to be untrue. This story came to mind when I was reading the article in *Savvy Times*, especially when I read the following: "We see what we want and we go for it. And being mechanically oriented, humans tend to apply more force rather than better psychology." (2) It seemed to me that the former FBI agent's use of rapport was a testament to the benefits of using better psychology rather than forceful techniques like waterboarding.

I am a classic task-oriented person. Crossing things off my to-do list is often the highlight of my day. However, almost every day my list is longer than I can possibly complete. I have found it necessary to balance my use of my list with giving myself a chance to stop and wait and respond, ensuring that important things get done that never get defined as a to-do. The article in *Savvy Times* was a great reminder about the importance of balancing these two approaches. While there may be times where the use of force or pushing to get things done is appropriate, there are also times where thoughtful choices might be a better way to go.

"Training horses naturally is all about balancing confidence and responsiveness, because if you are forceful and aggressive, you are likely to intimidate the horse and make him all sweaty and upset, and if you are loving and friendly without enough leadership, the horse will just take over…" (3) I know I'm not alone in finding that natural horsemanship techniques often apply equally well in the human world, too. For this task-oriented person, it's nice to know my study in one area of my life can do double duty!

(1)   Parelli, Linda. "What Does Your Horse Need?", *Savvy Times*, Issue 31, May 2011, Parelli Natural Horsemanship, Pagosa Springs, Colorado, p. 66

(2)   Parelli, p. 66

(3)   Parelli, p. 64.

APPROACH AND RETREAT

One night as I was heading out for last feeding, I had two things to dispose of outside. The first was a handful of carrot ends, whose destination was a pony's mouth. The second was an empty plastic box headed for the dumpster. As I walked out the door, I recognized these two items provided a teachable moment.

Ellie was finding many things in her new environment here unusual. She'd gotten used to the various machines. Then she found burning brush piles, lit after a heavy snow storm, a cause for concern. She expressed her concern with a loud snort first, followed by movement of her feet.

As I was walking past Ellie's pen on the way to the dumpster, I realized the plastic box presented an opportunity to desensitize Ellie to yet another element of her new life. The box was flimsy enough to move oddly, and it caught the shop lights in strange ways. Sure enough, when I approached Ellie and lifted the box for her to see, I got the expected snort, and she backed cautiously away. She then approached and retreated several times, getting closer to the box and sniffing each time. When she stayed with me (and the box),

she indicated acceptance of this new element of her environment. She greedily accepted the handful of carrot ends as her reward.

This short session presented a different version of approach and retreat as a training tool than I'd seen before. Normally I approach the pony and then retreat at a sign of stress, moving closer only when there is some relaxation and indication of acceptance. (I once saw this demonstrated when the first sign of stress was forty feet away, and this was in a domesticated horse!) The difference this time was that I stood still and Ellie did the approaching and retreating, showing me this is a very natural training tool indeed.

Horseman's Jingle founder Jerry Williams once shared that not only is approach and retreat appropriate for equines, it is also very important for us humans. The context of the conversation was loss of confidence after a setback in training or an accident. We humans sometimes work hard at getting our equines back on track, forgetting that we also need to work at getting our own confidence back. Jerry said that approach and retreat is an important tool for us, too, and we need to stop pushing ourselves through fear and instead honor that feeling and use approach and retreat with the situation that caused our lack of confidence.

After hearing Jerry describe the importance of approach and retreat for us humans, I realized I was unconsciously using it. I had a setback recently with one of my ponies, and while I had worked to help the pony recover, I hadn't thought to help myself. I had, however, retreated to spending time with my working ponies who are always there and waiting for me to ride or work. Being with them (especially since I trained them) builds my confidence so I can then approach my more challenging pony work. Now I see how approach and retreat has helped me regain confidence. I look forward to using it more consciously for confidence building in the future.

THE MAD ROMP

It all started because of a beaver.

One summer, I had Mya the Wonder Pony and her foal Aaron in a pasture that was divided into thirds by water. The first third, the West Bank, was divided from the rest of the pasture by the Michigan River. There is a shed on the West Bank, where I keep minerals for the ponies and where I expect to see the ponies congregating during the hottest part of the day. It took Mya a couple of weeks before she took Aaron across the river to graze for the first time. Aaron was no doubt thrilled with the adventure of crossing the river, as his yearling buddies had been crossing the river all summer without him.

Across the river, a swale divided the remaining pasture in two. In past years it held water early in the summer and gradually dried out as irrigation of the adjoining hay meadows ceased. Over the winter I had noticed that water was still standing in the swale, though, and it became evident that beavers were active downstream, causing water to back up in the swale. It took Mya another week before she took Aaron across this swale. Usually, though, she brought him back across the swale and then back across the river to the shed for part of the day.

One day I noticed that she wouldn't bring Aaron back. When I went to investigate, the yearlings were even hesitant to cross the swale. When I looked more closely, it was clear why: the beavers had apparently been industrious and had raised the water level by six inches in just two days. Yearling Meg was up to her belly crossing the swale to greet me, and Aaron would have had to swim to cross it.

227

The weather was mild, there was cover, and as water was readily available (!), I didn't worry for the first few days about Mya and Aaron being 'trapped.' Soon, though, the grazing ran out. The eastern pasture was the ponies' next destination, and it was accessible through a gate in the fence, so when I realized that Mya and Aaron were out of grazing, I opened the gate and urged all five ponies through.

About an hour later I went to check on Mya and her four younger charges. I was surprised at first that I couldn't find them, until I discovered an open gate on the far side of the pasture. Tracks indicated that the herd had headed north, though one set of tracks only went a short way then headed back south again. Fortunately, the pasture I lease is within a larger ranch whose perimeter is fenced. My concern for the ponies being loose was therefore somewhat relieved. Still, there were about 1700 acres left on which to find them!

I followed the tracks about a mile north along a forest road to a hay meadow where I lost them. I walked another half mile to the north edge of the hay meadow where there was a fence. I didn't find any tracks near the two open gates in the fence and was pondering how I might find the tracks again when I caught a glimpse of Rand, another yearling, standing on a sage bluff overlooking the meadow. I headed up onto the sage bluff and south again towards where Rand had been. It was clear he was in high spirits as he disappeared shortly after I saw him.

Before long I spied ponies in the hay meadow and headed down toward them. I wasn't sure what to expect since their spirits were likely still high from their mad romp, so I was elated by what happened next. When I called out to the ponies, four heads turned in my direction. I called again, and Meg started at a

228

gallop towards me. Then Rand started running toward me, then wee Aaron left his mother and started toward me as well. It was so gratifying to see these ponies come to me so eagerly when they had so many other choices they could make.

Meg, Rand, and Aaron followed me to Mya's side, still in high spirits, occasionally bucking and running around. I haltered Mya, then I began to look around for Matty, the fifth pony of this herd. She was rarely far from Meg and Rand and had developed a liking for Aaron and Mya, so I was surprised that she didn't appear. I hopped on Mya's back and headed south towards the pasture, calling to Matty as I went. Were it not for concern about Matty, I would have been enthralled with riding one pony with three others willingly gallivanting alongside on a beautiful late summer day. As it was, I at least had the presence of mind to recognize how fortunate I am to share my life with these ponies.

A half hour after putting Mya and crew back where they belonged and searching for Matty farther afield, we discovered that those tracks that had turned back were indeed hers. She was in the pasture where she was supposed to be and was happy to be reunited with her friends. The first picture shows the mad rompers a few days after their adventure, happily eating their vitamins. The second picture diagrams the mad romp on a photo taken the year before when Lily and I went on a pack trip up Custer Mountain.

FOAL WATCH – THE BETTER KIND

One of my least favorite things about breeding ponies is losing sleep waiting for mares to foal. I know (and my husband can attest) that I get cranky when I don't get my sleep, and foal watch is usually guaranteed to keep me up at night. I felt very fortunate one year when two mares foaled during my waking hours so that I didn't lose any sleep for them.

One of the benefits of the first foal watch is the second one that follows. I get to watch the foals grow and change. Here are some of my favorite observations of my foals one year when I had four:

- Fall had arrived here in the high country. The morning after the first frost, Rosie was very anxious to get her hay. She pushed Rand, who is a month older and heavier, off her hay pile, complete with pirouettes, bucks, and spins. It was the first time I'd seen Rosie push any of the other foals around.

- Meg was the smallest foal of the bunch, a half-Fell out of Mya. Meg and Mya were in a herd with Torrin. Mya and Torrin have been frequent companions for many years, and generally speaking, Mya is the boss. One day I was talking to Torrin, and Meg came up to join us. I was a little surprised, as Meg was just two weeks old, and I hadn't realized how comfortable she was with "Uncle" Torrin and how independent of her mother she'd already become. I was about to be even more surprised at the cheekiness of this little filly. Normally when foals approach adults, they exhibit a submissive behavior of drawing back their lips and working their jaws, as if to say "I'm just a little grass eater; don't harm me." I expected Meg to exhibit that behavior as she drew closer to Torrin and me. Instead, as they came muzzle to muzzle, she nipped at Torrin, exactly as her mother does when exhibiting her dominance. I nearly fell over laughing. Meg was barely 30" and Torrin is 13.3hh!

- Rosie and Rand were across a wire fence one day from Beauty, the senior mare. The three were sniffing noses with the youngsters exhibiting the submissive behavior described above. Beauty was quietly sniffing for about ten seconds, then she laid her ears back and tossed her head. In unison, Rosie and Rand spun away from the fence and put distance between themselves and the boss mare. Beauty always amazed me at how easily she could assert her dominance without ever moving her feet.

- One week, a few friends stopped by while I was caring for the ponies and came into the pasture to meet them. I hadn't a halter with me, so I took off my sweater to lead first Mya and then Torrin to meet the guests. Meg of course came along with her dam. Lily and her foal Columbine were a ways off in the pasture. As we were talking to Meg and Mya, though, here came Collie, all by herself, to see who these new people were. I was very surprised at how independent she was from her mother. For the first two weeks, it was nearly impossible to get between Lily and Collie, so close did Collie stick to Lily's flank. Lily never did come to meet the guests, but Collie stayed right with us for the duration of our visit.

- Rand was a Norwegian Fjord Horse colt and the oldest foal. He regularly called to me when he saw me and came to greet me before any other pony. One day, my husband was doing fence repairs at dusk and heard Rand call to him. It seemed unusual to Don, so he went to say hello to Rand. Rand came to him as usual, but when Don turned to leave, Rand called again. Don realized then that Rand's dam Sue wasn't around. It was growing quite dark, so he walked the entire pasture and couldn't find Sue. Rand continued to call out. Don came home and got me, and we went back down to the pasture to search under moonlight. We found Sue stuck in an abandoned barn in the pasture (which is now tightly barricaded). Don now calls Rand a hero for attracting Don's attention to the problem.

The picture shows Rosie ingeniously scratching her belly on a willow branch, another moment of blessing during the second phase of foal watch!

231

Mya's Antics

One December day Mya made me laugh, which was a vast improvement. Two weeks and then a week before, my beloved twenty-year-old pony relapsed, showing some signs of colic but other signs that were more confusing. We rushed her to the hospital the first relapse, two hours away, but the vet was only able to treat symptoms. Thereafter, treating her and monitoring her occupied most of my free time. There was some correlation with cold and changing weather. Fortunately the weather turned warm, so perhaps that's what led to her antics.

I was in the round pen with Lily, after having put Mya out to graze. We had had enough sun and so little snow that on the south-facing slopes there was dry grass, which Mya seemed to especially like. And since she hadn't had much of an appetite, I was happy to be able to offer her something she was interested in eating. I let her graze loose, and when I returned to get her forty minutes later, she was always within twenty yards of where I left her. Not this day, though!

Lily and I had been in the round pen for about fifteen minutes when we noticed that Mya was about fifty yards to the north of us. We had left her one hundred yards to the west, so she had definitely moved beyond her normal range. And she was in an area where there was no grass to eat, so I knew she was up to something. Lily and I continued working then suddenly Mya came trotting up the hill toward us. When she reached our elevation, she broke into a gallop and kicked her heels into the air as she ran past us and down the driveway towards Torrin, who was calling to her.

I was of course thrilled to see her showing such exuberance. And I was curious where she would be and in what frame of mind she would be in when Lily and I finished and headed in the direction we had last seen her go. She was fifteen feet from where I originally left her, looking innocent, which made me laugh. She came to me to be haltered, and the rest of the outing was uneventful. But her antics kept a smile on my face the rest of the day. Definitely an improvement!

STOCKING CAP GAMES

On a snowy afternoon, the only outdoor activity involving ponies that I could get half-way excited about was trimming hooves. I could do this under cover without snow sliding down my neck, and it needed to be done anyway. It was Lily's turn, and her good Fell Pony hooves required enough effort that I had no trouble staying warm. At one point I even threw off my stocking cap because of the long slow circuit her feet required with the nippers.

Throwing off my cap reminded me of my trimming experience a few days before. How many games can a pony devise with a stocking cap on the head of their favorite human? Lily and Torrin came up with quite a number while I was trimming Mya.

I was being lazy when I went to trim Mya, so I tied her but didn't tie her friends. Lily and Torrin took full advantage of their freedom to 'help' me with my chore, mostly by playing games with my stocking cap. Sometimes they nudged my cap so it fell over my eyes. Sometimes they lipped it just enough so I could feel it move. Or they would lip it, then when that didn't get a reaction, they would lift it a little more, and then a little more. Only once did I let the game progress to removal of my cap.

COURTESY PAULA GUENTHER

Torrin, whose head is huge and heavy, came up with an ingenious game. He rested his muzzle lightly on my cap. Then he gradually relaxed, letting the weight of his head slowly increase on mine. This game didn't last long because his head is way too much for my scrawny neck to support.

234

When I was trimming Mya's fronts, just one of her friends could get to my hat. But the hinds, ah, that was a different matter – there was room for both of them to work on my hat from different directions.

I will admit that my hat usually has bits of hay on it, as feeding for me is a full contact sport. So it's possible that Lily and Torrin were interested in the possibilities my hat presented for sustenance. Truly, though, I think they were more interested in playing games than anything else. Yes, for safety, I should have tied them, but I would have missed the laughter and their sheer joy at getting reactions out of me. The picture shows me wearing a stocking cap with my mare Ellie since I of course didn't have a camera the day that Lily and Torrin were playing stocking cap games.

VERTICALLY CHALLENGED

Mya the Wonder Pony and I went on a ride into one of the timber sales our company was logging. We were very fortunate because this particular sale was right next door; making for a nice commute. All Mya and I had to do was head off down the driveway and then take a right turn.

When I worked in industry, the company I worked for went through a period when it did intensive training of employees about diversity: gender, race, sexual orientation, etc. It was a great experience, in part because it encouraged us to look at life from a different perspective. The training could be pretty heavy at times, though, so we all appreciated a light-hearted lesson about politically correct language. One example: 'short' people are 'vertically challenged.'

On my outing with Mya, she seemed very pleased at the start - perky walk, head up, ears alert – despite gusty winds. We hadn't ridden in several days, and I got the sense she enjoyed the attention. After we took the right turn into the sale, though, I noticed Mya becoming a little agitated – her head was up higher, her pace was a little erratic, and she was looking anxiously from side to side. I thought it was the wind, but we'd had wind when we started, so that didn't explain it. Then I noticed one thing that had indeed changed. The snow banks on either side of the road were higher. They were so high, in fact, that she couldn't see over them;

I'm sure she felt like she was in a tunnel. Sure enough, when we got to a more open area where the banks were lower, she didn't seem as anxious anymore.

At 11.2hh, Mya is plenty of pony for me, though people comment that I look funny riding her with my long legs hanging way down. I only got larger ponies when eighteen inches of snow nearly immobilized Mya, and I couldn't keep my feet up out of the snow when riding her. On our woods ride, from my perch on her back, I could see that the snow out in the harvested areas of the forest was nearly four feet deep, definitely higher than Mya's back. Like the diversity training so many years ago, our ride helped me see the world from Mya's perspective. It's quite amazing, actually, that this was only the second time in the twelve years we'd been together that I could remember Mya being troubled by being vertically challenged. Her big heart makes her seem larger in all the ways that really matter.

IT'S A HUMAN THING

I grab my pony's head with hands firmly clapped to the jowls, arms outstretched, and plant a kiss on the fleshiest part of the muzzle. I then release my pony, and say "Sorry, it's a human thing..."

Usually I try to interact with my ponies in ways that respect them, recognizing, for instance, their need to not feel trapped. Clasping their head between my hands (enabling a kiss) or encircling some body part with my arms (a hug) is less than respectful behavior on my part. But sometimes I revert to strictly human expressions of affection. Sometimes I just can't resist giving a pony a big hug or a kiss.

Fortunately, my ponies are generally tolerant of my human displays of affection. One day I did the "clasp-the-head-plant-a-kiss" routine on two ponies in quick succession. Both of them 'licked-and-chewed' immediately, a sign to me that they accepted my very human communication. Another pony sought out some attention from me, and after she had accepted several scratches in her favorite places, I gave her a big hug around the base of her neck. She twined her neck over my back as if hugging back.

I've learned that human displays of affection are not always appreciated. I remember one extreme – after giving a pony a hug around the neck, the pony reached around and bit my thigh. This was early in my pony career, and I was quite disturbed by this reaction to my expression of fondness. I now understand how disrespectful I was on that occasion. Fortunately I've had numerous experiences on the other extreme. The picture shows my first stallion, Midnight, tolerating a mounted hug with no halter or leadrope.

238

I try to treat my ponies respectfully, blowing into their nostrils when they offer them, extending the back of my hand for sniffing as the first greeting, or petting them somewhere besides between the eyes where it's hard for them to see (especially the Fells whose forelocks obscure their vision.) But on those occasions when I'm overcome with my humanness, I follow my disrespectful act with, "Sorry, it's a human thing." And more often than not, I'm forgiven.

GIFTS FROM MADIE AND ROSE

In his book *Soul of a Horse*, Joe Camp says, "Many people have told me that if they let their horse live with a herd 24/7, they would lose their relationship with the horse. The horse would forget all about them. Ignore them. This is simply not true, if the relationship begins correctly in the first place. If the horse was allowed to make the choice to be with his human. If the human has proven to be a good leader." (1)

One summer day when we went to check on Shelley and her foal Madie, they met us at the gate as usual. Shelley was looking for a bucket with something interesting to eat in it, which we didn't have, and Madie was interested in the green grass under the gate. We gave each of the ponies scratches in their favorite places and checked them over to make sure they were all right. Then I walked out into the pasture to see how much feed remained for them. When I turned around, I saw Madie leave her mother and start walking with resolute purpose toward me. When she joined me, I scratched her several times in her favorite places and thanked her for her conscious effort to come see what I was doing. It meant a lot to me.

Madie is very special to us, so one day when we went to pasture to check on her and couldn't see her anywhere, we were instantly concerned. Finally I saw a tail flick up through the grass and could tell that she was lying down in a small depression that made her invisible from a distance. Don got to her before I did, and fortunately I did have a camera this time, so I snapped several pictures of the two of them while Madie was lying down then also when she got up. The two of them had quite a conversation, on Don's side at least about how worried we had been a few moments before.

Another day, when I was checking the larger herd at pasture, it was Rose's turn to touch my heart. No ponies were visible when I first arrived; Rose was the first pony to emerge from the willows when I called. I scratched her in her favorite places then checked each of the other ponies in turn. Rose was right at my elbow, eager to distract my attention from the other ponies. Jonty hadn't yet come to see me, so I began walking toward him, a few hundred feet away. Before long I heard steps behind me, and there was Rose. I greeted Jonty with a few scratches in his favorite places then greeted Rose again. Then I started back toward the rest of the herd, with Rose at my elbow. I stopped and scratched her again, then just to see how much she was 'stuck to me' I walked in a circle. Sure enough, she followed me around the circle. I could see she was questioning the sense of it, but she followed nonetheless. Rose's choice to be with me for those five minutes meant a lot.

Madie and Rose, living in their herds, chose to be with me instead of their herd for a few moments. By making a conscious effort to be with me, and even follow me, they showed me that I am a leader worthy of their respect. To have Madie, a three-month-old foal, tell me that was one thing, and then to have four-year-old Rose say the same was something else. Both gave me a great gift by their actions, that our relationship has meaning to them. My life is blessed by these ponies.

---

(1) Camp, Joe. *The Soul of a Horse: Life Lessons from the Herd.* New York, Harmony Books, 2008, p. 66

SNUBBED AND CHOSEN

All I wanted was a short trail ride on my favorite pony as a reward for a hard day. I had just finished trimming another pony's hooves, the sun was going down, and I wanted to ride down the driveway to see what my husband had been doing all afternoon. I had a halter and leadrope in my hand and a smile on my face as I approached her. She looked at me intently, then turned her head away. "Ah," I thought, "playing hard to get." I took a few more steps to her, and stopped when she looked at me, suggesting that she come to me. After a few moments, she turned her head away and took one step away, too. Snubbed!

I wasn't alone as I approached her though. Another pony was at my elbow, trying to stick his head in the halter. Even the pony whose hooves I'd just trimmed had expressed interest. But the pony at my elbow was especially persistent. Sometimes I'm slow, but I finally realized that while my favorite pony had snubbed me, this second pony had chosen to be with me even when I tried to ignore him. Apparently I was meant to take him for a ride that day.

I've had Torrin since he was two, and he has always done whatever I've asked of him in terms of work: skidding logs, pulling a sled or a forecart, and packing fencing supplies. He's not a mellow ride, though, which is what I thought I needed that day. And he's especially not mellow when food is on his mind. 'Fresh' is a term I think of when I argue with the ponies over my agenda versus their interest in food, especially in the spring when new green grass is a major distraction. Torrin felt pretty 'fresh' to me that day, despite it being November, with lots of go. I felt like I was sitting on a barely contained bundle of energy.

We used to ride a road where there was an ice-chest-sized rock with two round black rocks embedded in it. I thought of it as a rock with eyes, and Torrin always considered this a threat, no matter how many times a week we rode past it. During the winter he sees similar threats in spots of mud embedded in plowed snow. So I kept talking to him, and he stayed confident and well behaved and still full of energy as we briskly walked down the road.

Torrin was great until we turned around to come back up the road. A few strides towards home, and Torrin dipped his head and rounded his back, something he'd never done before. 'Oh boy,' I thought, 'I'm gonna experience something new.' Torrin's never bucked me off, but I thought my first was in store. I spoke sharply to him and he raised his head, evened out his back, and resumed forward motion. He was still full of energy but didn't share any other antics.

A little bit before home, I started asking Torrin for some sideways steps, changes of direction, and back ups, still mounted. He was immediately compliant and responsive. It was fun! He was right there, willing and interested despite not getting much attention from me in a long time. I don't know what I've done to deserve such a good boy. I'm sure glad I got snubbed and let him choose me!

MORNING ARRIVALS

One morning as I was doing chores at the top of the farm, three residents of the bottom of the farm came galloping up the road. Mya, Torrin, and Lily were in high spirits after their run, and they of course energized the upper farm herds with their arrival. I enjoy seeing my friends in high spirits, and I also really appreciate that they come down fast enough that I can walk up to them and halter them then tie them while I investigate what brought them to the top of the hill.

I'm sure they were pleased that my husband had already plowed the road, as the eighteen inches of snow we'd had in the previous twenty four hours would otherwise have slowed their progress to the top of the farm. It turns out that that snow was indeed the reason for their arrival, as it had buried the electric fence then snapped it, and my friends walked over the wire. That was probably the only thing they did slowly, since they knew I was feeding at the top of the farm and were undoubtedly anxious to get a piece of the action.

LILY AWAITING FENCE REPAIR

It was fun to have my three work ponies closer by while I was doing chores. And it was especially handy when it came time to do fence repair, as I was able to jump on Mya and head down the hill. We picked up a snow shovel on the way, a task quite similar to the ridden skidding we started with so many years previously. In hind sight I wished I'd also taken snowshoes, as the snow over the fence was up to my waist, so digging out the fence proved more of a chore than I had bargained for.

I ended the fence-repair chore by taking the remaining morning arrivals back to their paddock, ponying Lily from Torrin. I hadn't ridden 'T' in awhile, and it was a treat to find him as responsive as ever to my guidance, especially bareback with a halter and leadrope. It's always nice to get some enjoyment out of an unplanned chore!

THE LONG WALK

The last Saturday night of January in 2011, Mya and I took a long walk. It wasn't something either of us particularly wanted to do, but it was necessary. When I fed right before bedtime, Mya didn't meet me at the gate like she usually does, and she wasn't interested in hay. Then I watched her wander off and lay down and roll; very unusual behavior. She wasn't interested in treats, and she ran away from me, also very unusual behavior. A few minutes later when she had no interest in a bucket of feed, I immediately feared I was dealing with a case of colic.

This pony is my best friend and love of my life, so there was no question what needed to happen next. I returned to the house for a halter and lead rope, and we headed up the driveway. Our first stop was for a 10cc dose of the probiotic that I have had great luck with in cases of colic. Then we walked down the driveway and back up again for another dose of probiotic. We kept this pattern up for five to ten circuits, then we just walked. We started walking at 9:30pm and we finished walking at 4:30am when she finally showed interest in hay.

For the first three hours, I gradually saw small signs of improvement. One of them was her pace. When we started, she would walk very quickly, unusual behavior for this mellow pony. When she slowed to her normal pace, I assumed we were making progress. Other signs of improvement included her blowing out vigorously or licking and chewing as though there was some release of pressure. My optimism disappeared, though, around 1:30 when she seemed to take a sudden and certain turn for the worse. Her walking alternately sped up and slowed down and she gave indications of wanting to roll again. I realized that the skies had cleared and the temperature dropped ten degrees; I had heard stories of colic being triggered by changes in weather, and here I was witnessing it firsthand. My position on the lead rope took on a new urgency.

Right before I went out for that last feeding, I had read a chapter in *A History of British Native Ponies* by Anthony Dent and Daphne Machin Goodall. My friend Judith Bean loaned this book to me, and what a blessing it was that night. That chapter talked about the Epona horse-goddess cultures of northern Europe, and I decided it couldn't hurt to pray to Epona to spare Mya's life. And I called out to people who knew and loved Mya to send their prayers to help Mya get better. We watched Orion set in the west, and I talked to Mya about the stars overhead. I used my morning greeting call to her to communicate my love and concern for her, and I reminded her that she had survived the pain of labor and a previous post-foaling episode of colic. All of these things, I know, were as much for me as for her. They kept me from darker thoughts: would I have the energy to keep walking until Mya was better? I had been exhausted at 9pm and I certainly wasn't much improved at 2am. Would I get too cold (the temperature was around ten degrees Fahrenheit) and not be able to keep walking and possibly lose Mya because I was too weak? So I talked to Mya and I prayed, and we kept walking.

Around 3am, Mya finally passed some manure. Usually this is great cause for celebration in cases of colic, but she didn't give other signs of feeling better. She still wasn't interested in hay, nor showing any interest in her surroundings. So we kept walking. All told, we walked between seven and ten miles that night, up and down the driveway on packed snow. About an hour later she started looking towards her paddock-mates whenever we passed them on our walk. I counted this as a positive sign, and sure enough she showed interest in some feed soaked with the probiotic and then some hay. I watched her eat for forty-five minutes while I prepared a straw bed in a shed for her, and at 5:15am as the eastern sky was just beginning to lighten, I felt it was safe for me to go to bed.

While my concern for Mya was a motivation to keep walking, I have to give credit to my loyal canine companion, Sadie. This Australian Shepherd stayed with us all night up and down the driveway. At the house at the top of each circuit, she looked at me quizzically to make sure we were really headed out again, and I wouldn't have blamed her for laying down and trusting that I'd be back again in twenty minutes. But she didn't; she walked and trotted along beside us, occasionally taking a detour to see if there were fresh tracks of any kind. I don't know what I've done to deserve her devotion.

Even a week later, I was still a little anxious when I approached Mya's paddock until I saw her waiting for me at the gate. Then I could relax and enjoy her insistence that I feed her a treat. I could appreciate that she is still with me and that it's possible our long walk (and heavy doses of probiotic) saved her life. While I was exhausted and sore for a few days thereafter from our long walk, it was a small price to pay for all she has given me and the chance that she will give me even more in the days and years to come. If necessary, I know I'll take another long walk with Mya, probably praying to Epona, hoping for another recovery, and calling to all Mya's friends for assistance.

Solace

One night I was feeling low when I went out for last feeding. After I threw hay for the six ponies in the turnout, I leaned against the fence and let out a heavy sigh, looking at the moon and pondering my troubles. Within just a few moments, I felt a presence by my side. Rose had left her pile of hay and joined me. I took great solace from her presence as well as feeling touched that she would make the effort. For a few minutes I scratched her in her favorite places then let her go back to her hay - before her paddock-mates ate it all!

An acquaintance told me a related story that I doubt I will ever forget. Ginny is faced with a challenging health condition that impacts her mobility. She felt she needed to give up the equines in her life because it just didn't make sense to keep them when she wasn't using them. She and her family sold them all, 'only to find out I couldn't survive without the smell of a horse nose.' Ginny got a working pony, and the stories she told me about Sadie made me smile from ear to ear.

At one point Ginny got discouraged about her health problems and put Sadie up for sale. She had numerous inquiries, but she 'ran across Pat Parelli saying, "It's not about the riding...it's about the relationship." 'I decided he was right. She was the only thing that gave me any real enjoyment, and my husband and daughter did not want me to sell her.'

When Rose came up to me that night as I was wallowing in my trivial problems, I remembered Ginny and Sadie. Like Ginny, I'm not sure I can live without the smell of a pony nose. When I first got a pony, it was all about doing. Now, having ponies is for me as much about the relationship as it is about accomplishing things. On occasions like that night, when Rose showed she knew I needed some solace, I am reminded that my investment in our relationship pays dividends greater than I ever imagined.

MY WEEK TO LEARN FROM

One week, I had more need for emergency veterinary assistance than in my past twelve years of equine ownership. I have come to call it 'my week to learn from.' My vet told me I was making up for lost time. I'm afraid I didn't appreciate his sense of humor. While walking colicky ponies and on long drives to veterinary hospitals, I did a lot of wondering about why this all happened. The answer that emerged surprised me.

My husband is a battalion chief in our volunteer fire department. He also is involved with Search & Rescue.

It is not uncommon for emergencies to come in groups of three. One week a run of three included a car accident, a snow machine accident, and lost cross-country skiers. So at the beginning of 'my week to learn from', when we had one crisis in our business and one pony come down sick, I figured a third incident was soon to follow. What I wasn't prepared for was two sets of three.

After the week was over and I had a little more time to search for answers, I asked a friend for advice. She'd had a more tragic set of three the previous summer. She responded, "The universe is so much more powerful than what we can ever understand. Sometimes no matter what we do, and how hard we try, accidents and tragedy will happen."

The next day I found a new post on my nephew's blog. He shared this quote from Evelyn Underhill's *The House of the Soul and Concerning the Inner Life*: "Consider that wonderful world of life in which you are placed, and observe that its great rhythms of birth, growth, and death—all the things that really matter — are not in your control. That unhurried process will go forward in its stately beauty, little affected by your anxious fuss. Find out, then, where your treasure really is. Discern substance from accident."

The first thing that I related to was 'anxious fuss,' since anxiety was definitely something I was experiencing. Then I re-read the quote, and 'wonderful world of life' resonated, as indeed I am blessed to live in a beautiful place with many beautiful animals as companions. As a breeder of livestock I also had to notice 'great rhythms of birth, growth, and death,' for indeed this vocation is inherently about 'the things that really matter.' And then, finally, 'not in your control' sprang to the fore. I wanted to blame myself for the ills that came upon my ponies. The reality, though, was that factors beyond my control probably had as much or more to do with 'my week to learn from' than my actions did. A few factors that were at work were challenging winter weather, the position of an unborn foal in a mare's abdomen, and a tussle between two ponies over a pile of hay that resulted in one pony getting kicked in the head.

My nephew's blog post was titled "T'is the gift." I greatly appreciated this reference to a song that I had enjoyed years ago but had forgotten about: "T'is the gift to be simple, t'is the gift to be free..." I think my first encounter with it was the same as my nephew's, at the Quaker church his family attended in his youth. Later in my life I encountered it again when I was exploring simple living in earnest. As I've recovered from the stress of 'my week to learn from', I've tried to commit the words to memory. I've been surprised how hard memorizing it has been for me. And it has made me ponder what simplicity looks like at this stage of my life.

In *Way of the Horse*, author Linda Kohanov observed that horses have a way of humbling animal communicators and elite horse trainers who focus on big-headed solutions. She told of her own experience of looking for a solution to a problem with a horse and finding it to be much simpler than what she expected.

A few days after my week to learn from, I spoke to my friend and mentor Joe, and when he asked how I'd been, I told him about my week. Joe expressed concern about me and about the ponies, and then he surprised me. He quickly saw a common theme in the three veterinary emergencies that my husband had also mentioned but I found hard to accept. "Your ponies want to be with you." Could it really be as simple as that? As time has passed since 'my week to learn from', it's been hard to find a better answer. Heeding Underhill's advice, I've decided this is where my treasure really is.

AN ANTIDOTE TO GRIEF

I was grieving the death of a friend's pony. To help me with my sadness, I decided to take a short trail ride on Mya, and it proved to be a good antidote, including several doses of laughter.

Our ride started with a different sort of experience, though, for after I haltered Mya and stepped out onto the driveway with her, we saw not too far down the road a cow and calf moose. Cow moose are known to be quite aggressive, especially when they have calves, so after mounting I approached the pair with some trepidation. The sun was behind them, and I thought I saw the hackles come up on the cow's withers, which in turn stirred my stomach juices a bit. Mya seemed not the least bit  concerned; we've encountered moose numerous times on our rides together. A few seconds later, the moose gave ground. Perhaps because I was mounted, she felt that the pair of us wasn't worth taking on, and we continued on our way. I am often envious of Mya's confidence.

It was from then on that laughter became the dominant experience of the ride. I was late for feeding time, and while Mya accommodates my desires for rides when she is hungry, she also takes every opportunity to snatch bits of grass on our outings. Sure enough, when we turned off the driveway onto the trail, her head went down but her feet kept moving. We played various games with me trying to keep her feet moving and her trying to get as many mouthfuls as possible. As these games have been a part of our relationship for a long time, past behaviors resurfaced such as her grabbing a mouthful and starting to trot in anticipation of me urging her forward. I didn't want to trot though, just walk, so I asked her to resume the slower gait, and we

251

continued on, with me smiling at her antics. It's always entertaining on those occasions when she pulls the grass up, roots and all, because then she swings it about trying to get rid of the root wad while retaining the edible bits.

My biggest laugh came when we approached a tuft of grass that was taller than her ears and she swung her head to one side and then the other, biting at it twice. The results of her effort ended up extending nearly three feet on either side of her mouth. She seemed quite pleased with herself. As the grass 'whiskers' slowly got shorter as we went on, I chuckled over and over again.

It's been recommended to me several times to spend time with my ponies to deal with tough emotions like grief, and the advice has turned out to be very well given. My heart was still heavy about the death of my friend's pony, but I was also glad to experience joy with the ponies that are still in my life.

TRAVELING AWAY

I rarely travel, but in 2011, I traveled away from home for three days of people-filled events. I knew it was going to be a shock to my system since on most days I see more ponies than people. I'm quite comfortable with this ratio of people to pony time. And I heard a radio program before I traveled that suggested why this ratio might be so comfortable for me. (1) The program discussed the parasympathetic nervous system, which was described as 'rest and digest' and as an antidote to the sympathetic nervous system that is described as 'fight or flight.' My ponies embody for me a 'rest and digest' approach to life, and people, to varying degrees these days, seem to prefer constant stimulation that borders on 'fight or flight.'

This trip was one of only a few in the previous ten years into which I hadn't somehow incorporated a pony-related event. As I was putting my computer into its traveling case that morning, I realized it would have to be my proxy for ponies this time. On it were all my photographs and videos of my friends, and I figured I could pull them up to access that 'rest and digest' frame of mind in what I anticipated would be an emotionally challenging few days. At the last minute I also grabbed a DVD from Parelli Natural Horsemanship. I rarely take time to watch them, but I figured being stationary for a couple of hours on an airplane might provide me with an opportunity. Lo and behold, the one I brought was a terrific demonstration of 'rest and digest' being an antidote to 'fight or flight.'

The video showed Pat Parelli working with a young Thoroughbred racehorse that had been deemed untrainable. For a racehorse the Thoroughbred had more whoa than go; no one had ever figured out how to motivate him. The video was eighty minutes, long enough to completely capture my attention and focus me on the moment-to-moment changes that this master horseman was able to elicit. It was the next best thing to being with my ponies, for it in turn elicited in me a 'rest and digest' frame of mind. I'm sure my occasional chuckles were noted by my seat mates. I'm bummed I ran my battery out of juice before the second leg of my journey or I would have watched another video!

There were many parallels between the points made on the radio program about the parasympathetic nervous system and my study of natural horsemanship. For instance, "If the body is upset, the mind can't think clearly." In horsemanship, this equates to getting a horse to use his brain rather than his feet, to use the thinking part of his brain rather than the reactive one. How you do this varies with the horse's personality, and it seemed to me that the reason the Thoroughbred on the video was deemed untrainable was because he had a different personality than most racehorses so he needed different motivation. It was fascinating to watch Parelli be quietly persistent about good ground manners with the horse who'd been allowed to get away with crowding into his handlers. Some of Parelli's work was done mounted on his twenty-year-old mare Magic, and she occasionally assisted in teaching the younger horse respect for her space, too! Slowly, over the course of their time together, Parelli and Magic were able to get the young horse to quit reacting and to think about what was being asked of him and then to get him to do things voluntarily that he'd previously refused to do.

The radio program also said that the brain has a "negativity bias, which is like Velcro for bad experiences but Teflon for positive ones." (2) It's therefore important to develop practices in one's life that undermine the brain's tendency to go negative. I have definitely found that interacting with my ponies, even if it's just hanging out time rather than working or training, helps in this department.

As my three days away from my ponies unfolded, I put some thought into how to hold onto the 'rest and digest' frame of mind that my ponies elicit in me. I know it's about retraining my brain to respond differently to stimuli, including people. I know my ponies will benefit if I can be successful, too. For, as the radio program said, "If you can change your brain, you can change your life." (3)

---

1)   http://www.newdimensions.org/flagship/3336/rick-hanson-a-brain-that-knows-how-to-be-happy/
2)   http://www.rickhanson.net/writings/buddhas-brain
3)   Same as #2

LAST FEEDING

It's a cold January night. The moon is high in the sky, bathing the snow in silvery light. I am outside one last time to feed my ponies before bed. At the first paddock, several youngsters line the fence, awaiting my arrival. I greet them with scratches on their foreheads, but I don't cross the fence. I await the arrival of the head mare, as I know she'll push the young ponies away and greet me with her usual question, "Treats?" After answering her question in the affirmative, I give her the biggest pile of hay after I enter the paddock, both because I know she needs it and because I know that no other pony will push her off it.

At the next paddock, my stallion awaits me at the fence, prepared for our greeting ritual. I rub his forehead and clear his thick forelock away from his eyes. How he sees anything through all that hair is beyond me. I may ask him to back away with a wiggle of my finger or a single spoken word, or I may scratch one of his favorite places. He is looking for some way to engage me in a game. Tonight it's enough to walk to the haystack together, stopping, backing, and turning in unison, he and I, until he runs one of the mares off, proclaiming me his own. When I approach with the tub of hay, he backs away and awaits permission to eat.

At the final paddock, my first pony, and still the love of my life, awaits me at the gate and nickers her soft greeting. I can't even face the thought of her not being in my life. I ask if she'll take me for a ride tomorrow, and she licks and chews her answer. I'm glad these ponies live to ripe old ages! I call the younger mare to me, feed her a treat and rub her forehead. When she tosses her head, I tell her she's definitely her mother's daughter (the boss mare from the first paddock.) Here, I spread the hay in several different piles, as the neediest pony is the lowest in the hierarchy, so when the fast-eating gelding finishes his first pile and pushes the young mare off her pile, there's another pile for her to go to.

As I head back to the house with all the feeding chores done, I pause in the bright moonlight to tell the ponies I love them. And it comes to me that they're all willing to try for me; I just need to ask. Some I have asked more from than others. The others await me. One lifetime will certainly not be enough.

255

KNOW YOUR PASSION; ENGAGE IT DAILY

I was asked once to share something I've learned from the life that I commenced after retiring from my first career. Here is what I came up with after reflecting on the farming life I adopted: know what you're passionate about and engage in it daily.

Farming by its nature has its cycles and ups and downs. One of my early mentors reminded me that along with livestock, for instance, there's deadstock. Not easy to deal with, but part of the territory.

Most of us get involved in farming because it's something we're interested in but also for other, more deep-seated, reasons. My particular interest is in sustainable agriculture and the role that rare breeds can play in sustainable systems. In particular, my passion is working ponies. I have found that I can weather the ups and downs of farming better if I interact with a pony in some way every day.

As I've pondered sustainability, I've become convinced that passion is a key part of the picture. For me, sustainability has the three legs of the triple

bottom line: social, economic, and ecologic or environmental. Passion fits in the social leg; I'm convinced it's an absolute requirement for a future that generations to come will want to inherit.

Sometimes we don't take time to identify exactly what we're passionate about. I am married to a man who has been clear about his passion since he was a teenager and has figured out how to live it ever since. I tell him he's unusual; that most people can't see their own passion as clearly as he does. He finds that hard to believe. I'm living proof of taking the long road, of course, as I'm now on my third 'career'. This one has lasted longer than the other two because I finally found what feeds my soul. I've watched other people

256

bounce around in life from one thing to another, clearly searching for their passion. They've helped me understand that it's worth the time to figure out what moves us and to hang on once we find it, if for no other reason than to avoid wasting precious life energy bouncing around.

Several years ago I cut a saying out of an advertisement. It reads, "If no one else shares your level of passion, you are where you belong." When the going gets rough, I re-read this saying. Because my passion is my unique contribution to the world, staying focused on it reduces stress, minimizes tension in relationships, and renews my determination. I would have quit long before now if I weren't passionate about what I'm doing.

Another quote I've found helpful about passion is from E.O. Wilson, the renowned biologist. It too suggests that following your unique calling in life can be a lonely road but is nevertheless an important one. "You are capable of more than you know. Choose a goal that seems right for you and strive to be the best, however hard the path. Aim high. Behave honorably. Prepare to be alone at times and to endure failure. Persist! The world needs all you can give." Enough said.

I have not attempted to provide an authoritative guide to partnering with ponies because such a work isn't possible. Instead I've provided stories that reflect what partnering with a pony can look like. In particular I've told stories that reflect how I have partnered with my ponies so far. I already know that there are more stories to be told.

For instance, in 2015:

- While I quit riding her a few years ago, Mya's work ethic in harness still amazes me.
- I now have her mild recurrent colic stabilized, which began after she was kicked in the head.
- Torrin did a skidding job this summer. He still reaches for his bit.
- Both Mya and Torrin did something this fall they'd never done before as pack ponies.
- I have a new chore-pony-in-the-making in Rose who has started hauling manure for me. Working Rose is a special thrill because I bred her, raised her, and trained her.
- Madie has returned after three years with another owner. I am enjoying renewing our relationship and exploring what our partnership might evolve into.
- New research is published all the time that pertains to stewarding the health of ponies. Some of the research is actually now about ponies, not just horses!

I continue to learn from my herd, at work, play, in breeding, and husbandry. Partnering with ponies is indeed a journey, not a destination. It is abundantly clear that one lifetime will not be enough.

OTHER BOOKS BY JENIFER MORRISSEY

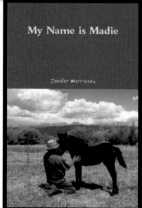

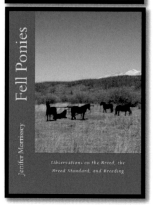

ISBN #: 0692308555

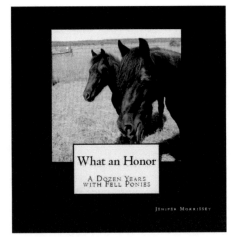

- *A lot of love shines between the lines, so we learn from you with a smile and a warm feeling. I like that you learn so much from a book that is entertaining AND non fiction.* – Antje Assheuer
- *I have nothing but good vibes coming from my reading.* – Judith Bean

Jenifer Morrissey brought home her first pony at Thanksgiving in 1998 and has been grateful ever since. She has a Bachelors degree in Electrical Engineering from Stanford University and a Masters degree in Environmental Policy and Management from the University of Denver. Her articles have appeared in *Rural Heritage*, *Driving Digest*, *Small Farmers Journal*, and *Heavy Horse World* magazines. She raises rare breeds of livestock and owns a logging and construction business, Focused on the Forest, LLC, with her husband in Gould, Colorado.

Made in the USA
Lexington, KY
15 November 2017